[CONFIDENTIAL]

FORBIDDEN KNOWLEDGE COLLEGE

MICHAEL POWELL

Published by Adams Media, a division of F+W Media, Inc.
57 Littlefield Street
Avon, MA 02322
www.adamsmedia.com

ISBN 10: 1-4405-0457-1
ISBN 13: 978-1-4405-0457-0

Printed in China

This publication is designed to provide accurate and authoritative information
with regard to the subject matter covered. It is sold with the understanding
that the publisher is not engaged in rendering legal, accounting, or other
professional advice. If legal advice or other expert assistance is required,
the services of a competent professional person should be sought.
—From a Declaration of Principles jointly adopted by a Committee of the
American Bar Association and a Committee of Publishers and Associations

Many of the designations used by manufacturers and sellers to distinguish
their product are claimed as trademarks. Where those designations appear in
this book and Adams Media was aware of a trademark claim, the designations
have been printed with initial capital letters.

Photographs by BigStockPhoto.com and Istockphoto.com
Illustrations by Allen Boe and Istockphoto.com
Design by Allen Boe

This book is available at quantity discounts for bulk purchases.
For information, please call 1-800-289-0963.

FORBIDDEN KNOWLEDGE COLLEGE

INTRODUCTION:

There are lots of college books that tell you how to do stuff that you really should know how to do, like how to choose a course or survive your freshman year. But have you ever wondered about the things that you really should NOT know how to do, like how to binge drink on a budget, major in laziness, plagiarize without getting caught, or treat your folks like an ATM?

Do you know how to find a campus booty call, sell your organs for beer money, swallow a goldfish, hack the library computers, or kidnap the Dean? Now we're not suggesting that you go out and start being a lawless troublemaker, but that doesn't stop you from being curious about how it's done, right? This book has been written in the same spirit as one might sell a chainsaw to a brain surgeon—the information will pique your curiosity, but we hope that you'll never have occasion to use it.

In this outrageous handbook, 101 college related activities are subjected to impartial peer review, from the ridiculous to the downright illegal. Many are about living it large; some are dangerous; others will get you arrested, injured, or, worse yet, expelled—it takes you on an intellectual, emotional, physical, and spiritual odyssey beyond reason without stopping for pee breaks to experience moral and philosophical challenges that are so out there that you'll never need to consult a course syllabus again.

ACCEPTED

CONTENTS

1. Choose a Party School:

College is life's way of saying, "Let's party!" So, high-octane partying should be your top priority when choosing one. You have the rest of your life to get an education or become a corporate drone, but never again will you have the opportunity to get blitzed in the company of thousands of your peers.

What Is There to Do Around Here?

Visit a potential college, grab some students and ask, "What is there to do around here?" The only answer you want to hear is: "Nothing else but friggin' party man. You look thirsty. Would you like one of my beers?"

An exception to this rule is University of California Santa Barbara, which also offers chilling on a beach—awesome. That means getting buzzed on sand, dude. Check it out. On the flipside of the weather, places like Montana State that get snowed in up in the mountains become true party schools out of necessity—plus they have really cold beer. Alternatively, head into the sticks—at those colleges everyone grows their own weed.

What's Your Scene?

Decide what kind of party scene you enjoy: on campus, at the bars, or tailgating around a big game—or all of the above. If you visit at 2:30 P.M. on a Tuesday afternoon and everyone is trashed, then you've truly hit party gold.

At big football colleges, partying is focused on tailgating before and after the Saturday game. However, at some football schools many students wise up and only really go for the fourth quarter. And at schools like Florida State, where most of the games are at night, you can spend the whole day getting wasted.

If the town doesn't have at least thirty rocking bars, preferably on the same street, then choose a college with a bigger town. Also the bars need to stay open well into the morning.

For a wild frat party scene you can't get much better than DePauw University (Greencastle, Indiana) or Washington and Lee University (Lexington, Virginia). If you like getting wasted in the dorms, you can likely find that at any college. Check out some of the bigger state schools where there are so many students the RAs will have a hard time tracking you down.

Putang and Pizza

Lots of colleges boast the hottest women, but if you drink enough beer nearly ALL the women are hot. And make sure local pizza delivery runs 24-7. Because nothing beats a large pepperoni after a night of drinking and hooking up.

Special Events

Major holidays like Halloween must be a total blur. Ohio University has an insane Halloween party. And at UConn (University of Connecticut), Spring Weekend sees 50,000 drunken revellers packing into a huge parking lot with hundreds of kegs. Ask around and unless the college throws the kind of events where the police have to close down ten blocks, take your business elsewhere.

2. Write the Best Admissions Essay Ever:

Year after year competition for spots at the top schools gets harder: Harvard rejects about eleven applicants for each one it accepts. Lots of students have similar backgrounds and grades, so a stunning admissions essay can make the difference between getting a place in the college of your choice, or growing old stacking shelves in your hometown. The sole purpose of your essay is to convince the admissions officer that you are what they want.

Answer the Question

If the essay is expected to answer an assigned question use it to demonstrate critical thinking and express your personality and your strengths with simple but expressive language. Show who you are, what you think, what you can offer, and why you chose that particular college. If you need to use a thesaurus, it's a warning that you have nothing much to say.

Keep It Real

Avoid extravagant claims, or cheesy aspirations (like your passion for world peace, or racial harmony, or how your courage and leadership helped your team win the state championship). Real achievements and genuine convictions should be expressed in an honest and direct way. Admissions staff only offer places to applicants they connect with, so anything that isn't an impressive yet personable version of the real you isn't going to cut it. Express appropriate personal details, but save your embarrassingly personal information like mental health problems and family tragedies for your *Real World* audition tape.

BU

Above all, be you. Don't be quirky or silly. Be original. There is nothing as refreshing as someone with the self-assurance to show who they are in a confident and open way. Avoid gimmicks and don't mention GPAs or standardized test scores. What makes you different from everyone else, and what are your major accomplishments, and why do they matter? Provide concrete examples to back up your argument.

Restrained Passion

Discuss your future goals and aspirations. If you have a passion, express it with charm and intelligence. Genuine enthusiasm is very memorable.

Spelling and Punctuation

Spelling mistakes and bad grammar will make you appear ignorant, period. Check and double check your work to remove all grammatical errors.

3. Ace Your Admissions Interview:

The admissions interview is your opportunity to show that they broke the mold when they made you—that you are a one-off, a nugget of gold in a dirty pile of panhandled slag, or at the very least, a limited edition. You'll get asked a bunch of achingly predictable questions, so prepare some original answers that reveal the real you. Oh, and be prepared to lie your ass off.

Tell Me About a Challenge You Overcame

Always make one up. Unless your mother is a crack whore and your father sells drugs on street corners, your major life challenges to date have only been what color pencil-case to buy, or which member of the Jonas Brothers you'd most like to beat up. Tell them you just ran with the bulls, or like Lindsay Lohan you managed to get all your rehab out of the way before you reached the legal drinking age. That's impressive.

Tell Me About Yourself

Here is a great open-ended softball you can whack into the bleachers. Tell them three amazing facts about yourself—you collect your toenail clippings; you play *Mafia Wars* for four hours every day; you keep a six-pound candle made from your own ear wax in your bedroom, etc.

Why Do You Want to Come to This College?

Be honest and explain that you are hoping to get laid plenty and then make lots of money after you graduate. They'll respect your honesty and your answer will stand out much better than talk of intellectual interests or the quality of the staff.

Whom Do You Most Admire?

Don't make the mistake of picking just one person—be original and expansive and choose an entire nation like "The French." You can bet nobody has said that before.

What Do You Want to Major In?

Here's your chance to enquire about the easiest majors, and which have the slackest policies on skipping lectures. Then tell them that you're only kidding—before picking a major you're going to take lots of classes and see which professor you develop the biggest crush on.

What Do You Do in Your Free Time?

Say you don't get time for hanging out and chillin' because you spend all your time studying. As college types who have spent their lives in academia, they'll relate to that; you'll sound like one of them.

Make Them Envy You, But Not Too Much

They are old and have missed most or all of their life chances; they are full of bitterness and regrets and then you appear, all bright eyed and young, your whole life ahead of you, not to mention more sex and partying than they have had in the last thirty years. On the one hand, they have the power to decide who the next generation of college students will be and they want you to succeed in the interview; on the other, they will zone in on any facet of your personality that reveals you to be undeserving of their benevolence.

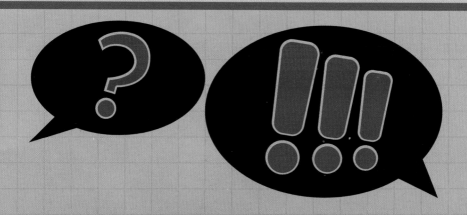

4. Lie Your Way into the Ivy League:

Ivy League acceptance is rife with nepotism, favoritism, inconsistencies, and superficiality, so there's always room for one more impostor. Lie about your GPA and SATs and then steal other people's identities to open up potentially unlimited streams of federal funding. The two most famous examples of this are Esther Reed and James Hogue. Reed was arrested in 2008, at the age of 30, after spending a decade attending Ivy League colleges using various aliases and the identity of a missing person. Hogue invented a persona that he knew would appeal to "Princeton admission committee's self-serving mythology of Ivy league diversity, inclusion and merit." Beware: This is a very sophisticated kind of fraud that requires advanced levels of acting skills and maybe even some computer hacking.

Assume an Identity

Look on missing persons websites to find a missing person, presumed dead (but not officially dead), who is approximately the same age as you. (Reed went one better; she gained access through State Police computers to a missing-persons database accessible only to law-enforcement officials.) Use their Social Security Number, name, and birth date to create an alternate persona. When applying for colleges, if anyone gets suspicious tell them that you are in a witness-protection program.

Alternatively, like Hogue, reinvent yourself as a self-reliant multicultural farm boy (Alexi Indris-Santana), "herding cattle by day, reading Plato by night" who presses all the right buttons with elite pseudo-liberals.

Fake Your ACT or SAT Scores

Hack into the ACT or College Board databases and enter a ACT score of 34 and SAT of 2300. Don't make them higher than that otherwise colleges will get suspicious.

Choose Your College

Reed conned her way into Harvard, Columbia, and California State University at Fullerton, and Hogue got into Princeton. Therefore they probably have introduced a vetting procedure so they don't get caught with their pants down again. But allegedly they haven't cooperated with the police, so if they were fooled once maybe they can be again.

Major in Deceit

Choose a major that can teach you more about being the ultimate con artist. Reed majored in Criminology and Psychology, but you might also like to try Law or Drama, since you'll also require sharp acting skills—a police investigator described

Reed as "an excellent impostor to the point of being patho-
logical."

Become an Expert Listener

The best way to hide your real identity is to show exag-
gerated interest in others. Most people love talking about
themselves, so if you become the perfect listener you won't
have to give out much information about yourself. According
to one source, Reed came across as "very interested in whatever you're doing, she talks to you about you, but provides
very little information on her own." Always line up people and
information that you can use to your advantage, so that you
can leap-frog to other identities and frauds.

Transfer After Your First Year

If fraud pushes you too far out of your comfort zone there
is a boring solution. Forget lying your way into the Ivy
League. Go to another college first and show dramatic improve-
ment at the college level from your average high school
achievements and then apply to transfer to an Ivy League
school. Though, where's the fun in that?

5. Con Your Way into an Athletic Scholarship:

An athletic scholarship can be a free ticket—the best ones (the "full ride" scholarships) pay tuition, books, travel, room and board and much more. But the great secret is that you don'thave to be top notch to get one. Sure, the top Division I schools will be way out of your league, but there are many ways to mop up the beer money flowing from lesser colleges' programs. Start early: Don't wait until your senior year in high school to do your research.

Nerds Welcome

You don't even have to be very good at sports to cash in because some athletic scholar-ships focus more on academic prowess and your drive than how far you can throw a football. And if you're a woman, gender equity means that scholarship providers are falling over them-selves to come into the 21st cen-tury. Your ethnicity and religion may also give you an advantage.

There are three main national athletic organizations that hand out wads of cash: the National

Collegiate Athletic Association (NCAA), the National Association of Intercollegiate Athletics (NAIA), and the National Junior College Athletic Association (NJCAA). Don't bother with the NCAA, unless you're Michael Jordan. Besides, you don't want to make athletics your career—you just want the money, right? Focus instead on the NAIA and the NJCAA, which offer lots more scholarships to screw-ups like you.

Special Interest Scholarships

You don't even have to be a jock to get a sports scholarship. Even the NCAA offers stuff like The Freedom Forum NCAA Sports Journalism Scholarship Program for students who are passionate about being sports journalists. The best way to con the trustees that you are a passionate journo is to learn lots of NCAA facts and stats, *Rain Man*-style. Nothing impresses them more than someone with a bunch of pointless statistics at their fingertips. In many cases dedication to the sport is more important than ability. Fake commitment to your sport and you're half way there.

Pick an Emerging Sport

Emerging sports attract hand-outs too. Forget baseball, basketball, and football. Choose a minority or emerging sport like archery, badminton, bowling, squash, synchronized swimming, beach volleyball, or water polo. Also, did you know that The National Intercollegiate Rodeo Foundation offers a number of $1,000 scholarships each year to the most obsessive Garth Brooks fan?

6. Pack for College in Three Minutes:

Trying to decide what to pack can be more stressful than bribing your way into college in the first place. But you can cut down the whole business to about three minutes by following this simple rule: Packing is knowing what to leave out. You don't need to include everything for the whole academic year (except toiletries, which you can get your parents to pay for). Besides, within a week you'll be stealing your roommate's clothes, laundry detergent, shower gel, and bath shoes. Here are the essentials:

Condoms

You can't go wrong if you shield your dong. Buy a twelve pack and take three out. Nothing shouts "virgin" louder than a pristine box of shrink-wrapped johnnies.

Clothes

Only pack clothes that can be machine washed and tumble dried—enough for two weeks, plus one smart outfit and lots of hangers. Bring a metal laundry basket with a tight-fitting lid to keep odors locked away until you can be bothered to wash your clothes. This will help to stop your room from smelling of stale beer and vomit.

Quarters

Everyone needs quarters, but few are smart enough to bring five thousand of them. Hide your stash, but always keep three quarters on your person at all times; then when someone begs you for some for their laundry, you can give them your "last three" in exchange for a dollar (for the inconvenience). They'll soon forget that you owe them a quarter. By the time you've emptied your stash you'll have made a profit of $1,250.

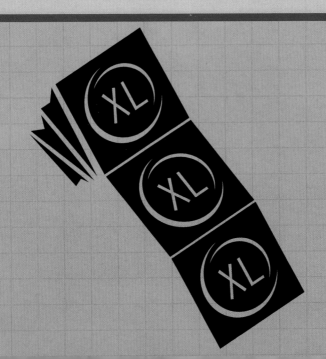

Power Strips

Because it is a proven fact that whoever designs dorm rooms hates wall outlets.

Mini-fridge

Coordinate with your roommate and make sure he brings the microwave if you bring the fridge, because microwaves always get broken by dumbass student experiments. Also, you get to prioritize what gets chilled (food or beer).

Laptop

When you finally get around to doing some work (i.e. downloading music and movies), a laptop is a must. If it's new, don't pay a premium to have programs installed, as most colleges will give you Microsoft Office for free. If not, there are plenty of free web-based versions of applications with similar capabilities. Make sure your laptop has a physical lock plus some kind of electronic tracking or locking device.

Wall Posters

Don't bother trying to be original or kooky with your choice of wall decoration. Play it safe. Who do you think gets more action: the jock who plasters his walls with clichéd choices like John Belushi, The Periodic Table of Mixology, Shelby Mustang GT500, Beer Pong Rules, George Costanza spread out on a couch in his underwear, a guy surfing a 30-foot wave OR a self-harmer with a prized collection of My Chemical Romance lithographs?

7. Break Up with Your High School Sweetheart:

Troy and Gabriella may have made the transition from high school to college, but in reality it's best to make a clean break right after the cherry-popping prom, so at college you're free to rack up more one-night stands than Tucker Max. Going steady after high school sends all the wrong signals. When you find yourself hitched with a job and a baby while in college as all your friends are getting aneurisms from boning themselves stupid, it's your own fault. Breaking up is never painless, so inflict maximum pain for the greatest closure.

Don't Break Up by Text or Email

That is so last-decade and wastes time. Simply Tweet, or change your Facebook status to "single."

Manage Your Time

If you are forced to dump her face to face, make it clear that you have no intention of dragging out the conversation. Allow three minutes for each year you have been together, with a minimum time of a microwave burrito and a maximum of a pizza delivery, because if you've ever watched someone plead and blubber like a baby for forty-five minutes you'll know that it builds up an appetite. Don't bother offering food to your soon-to-be ex, as they won't be hungry and will probably feel fat and ugly right now.

Blame Yourself

"It's not you, it's ME . . . who thinks I could do a whole lot better than you and that you're not sexy enough."

Pay a Compliment

"You have a great body—it's just your face that is . . . well, you know. Also, you're way uglier than anyone I have ever dated before, and plan to date in the future, so that says a whole lot of good stuff about your personality, don't you think?"

Fresh Meat

Stress that you want to find someone better—that's why everyone breaks up. "We can still be friends, but don't call me. We should be the kind of friends who never call each other and never get in touch. If it's meant to be then we'll get back together again some day . . . after I've boned tons of girls more attractive than you."

8. Survive the First Week:

Everyone else may seem cooler and more confident than you but that's only because they are. So now's the time to reinvent yourself and be the happening hipster you never quite managed to be in high school—though if that's what you're thinking you're probably a lost cause. You can't escape who you really are, so relax, make some new friends, and have fun.

Lose the Lanyard

Hazing has been officially banned at many schools but it's still fairly common, and nothing says "I'm a loser freshman" better than the lanyard. Get rid of it and increase your cool rating by five hundred percent. And don't wear your Varsity jacket, fool.

Fitting In

Join lots of clubs, even the ones you have doubts about, and try to meet as many new people as possible. Don't glue yourself to one or two, or you'll reduce your options and maybe even turn others away by appearing needy or clingy.

Don't ask people what grade they are in—you're not in high school anymore. We say "year" now, and it's a kind of dumb freshman-type question anyhow. Inevitably people will ask you what you're majoring in, but try to think of more interesting questions to ask others.

First Impressions

Don't try so hard to fit in that you do something you'll regret for the rest of your college days. At the end of a night of hard drinking you may think that peeing in a cup of beer, drinking it, puking into the cup, and then pouring the contents over your head while your "friends" egg you on, is the way to go. They may be laughing at your antics now but tomorrow they'll sober up, remember what you did, and shun you forever. It is hard to shake a reputation made early on so make a good first impression. Some of the people you bond with in the first week will become lifelong friends, but you'll probably never talk to most of them again.

Live in the Present

Don't bore all your new friends with stories about how great your old friends back home are; you're only doing it to make yourself look cool, or to reassure yourself. Focus on your new friends. And if you were stupid enough to keep your high school sweetheart, don't spend hours on the phone with her, or you'll look unapproachable. If you need to call your parents to have a homesick cry, wait until your roomie leaves, no matter how much you think you've already bonded with him. Then get out of your room and go meet some more people. This week, when you're in your room, keep your door open.

9. Choose the Easiest College Major:

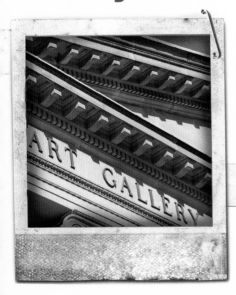

The easiest majors make you the least employable and the students who work their asses off in college will soon own the Maserati Quattroportes you'll be squeegying at the intersection in a few years time. It's a trade off. Party hard now, wash windshields in your thirties.

Avoid All These

The hardest majors are Chemistry, Mathematics, Physics, Engineering, Computer Science, Pre-Med, Pre-Law, and Architecture, or any combination of those like Chemical Engineering. You will spend all (and we mean ALL) your time—including evenings and weekends—studying.

Art History

With an art history degree you could maybe get a job cleaning the toilets at a museum or art gallery, and then in about ten years you'll have worked your way up to be the lonely fat guy two years away from congestive heart failure who barks at people not to touch the exhibits, or take photographs. But you'll have a great time at college, and you'll hang out with lots of rich kids whose parents own condos in Aspen.

Philosophy

Spend all morning smoking weed with your professors and discussing the nature of reality, and then disappear so far up your own navel that you actually begin to believe you can pick up women in bars with lines like, "Are you a phenomenalist or a relative realist?" You won't get laid, but at least you'll become aware of the futility of existence two decades earlier than your peers.

American Studies

Learn all about your own life, plus stuff you know already, like how to order at a drive-thru, or buy a gun in Wal-Mart. Watch *Forrest Gump*, eat at Taco Bell and Applebee's, and pass the course without attending any lectures.

CIS and Business Related Stuff

How to sell stuff to other people, taught by people who weren't very good at selling other people stuff themselves so e they ended up teaching people how to do it. Save yourself the trouble and go to the mall and laugh at all the zombies maxing out their credit cards on junk they don't need.

Sociology

Learn why some human beings shoot other human beings and how much like monkeys we all are. Break for lunch. Spend the afternoon playing football with all the other sociology jocks.

Theater Studies

This is any course where you learn about performance, or you actually perform stuff and get a bunch of people to watch you doing it and lie to you afterwards about how good you were. Enjoy the attention now because when you try to earn a living from this shit you'll spend the rest of your life wondering why your lecturers never told you that only the super-talented or the beautiful earn a decent living this way.

10. Find the Best Dorm:

You'll probably have to live in a dorm for at least your first year, as most colleges require it. Sometimes you luck out—if you go somewhere like Loyola College in Maryland, the rooms are palatial and you can make some extra cash by subletting the closet. At Scripps College in Claremont, CA, nearly all the students get single rooms and the common rooms have a grand piano and a fireplace. At Smith College in Northampton, MA, your dorm is a house.

Even if you can live off campus for your first year, you'll meet more people if you stay in a dorm, although the trade-off is less privacy and a fair share of douchebags with poor musical tastes.

Hall Reputation

Your college website and its handbook will give you a description of each hall, but that's the "official" line and you can only get the real picture by talking to students who are already there, so ask around. Each dorm will have its own character and you need to decide what kind of room will suit you best—a double, triple, or quad; single sex or co-ed, on or off campus. Choose a dorm that hosts lots of activities and attracts a variety of different people. If you're majoring in something like music, you'll meet plenty of like-minded people in your courses, so don't pick a special-interest dorm or you'll miss out on a wider social circle.

Single or Double

Most people have to share, so it's rare to get a single. Besides, you're never lonely with a roomie, even a jerk-off. Suites can be a riot, but the group dynamic means problems like personality clashes can be magnified as well, and it's not uncommon for one person to feel left out or victimized. The bigger the dorm the less sleep you're going to get.

Crappy Dorm

A crappy dorm is not always a bad thing because in a dump nobody will notice when you drill a few more holes, mark the walls, or accidentally pee in the closet, whereas in a pristine dorm you will have loads more prohibitive rules and a much harder time concealing any damage.

11. Live Rent Free:

After tuition and beer, rent is your biggest cost at college, but if you are smart you won't have to pay a cent for your accommodations. There are several possibilities that offer different levels of inconvenience in exchange for free board, from living with your parents to house-sitting a houseboat.

Live with Your Parents

This is the least desirable option for obvious reasons, but if your college is local then it is one way to save money. Only take this route if you really have no other choice, or as a means to an end (like if you are are saving to buy a house/start a business).

Get a House and Rent It Out

Rent or buy a house (getting your parents to act as co-signers) with at least four bedrooms and reserve the smallest room for yourself. Contact the utility company for the cost of running the utilities for a year, then divide the total annual running cost including rent or mortgage payments by 12 to get the monthly budget. Divide this figure again by the number of remaining rooms to get a rough monthly room rent, adjusted up or down depending on the relative size of each room, but making sure that it adds up to your total monthly budget.

Interview tenants, but don't be too picky. Take two months' rent upfront plus a security deposit (put the deposit in the bank and don't touch it) and get them to sign a simple statement of agreement committing them to a minimum of six months. Get Internet, but not a phone account—it's too complicated; everyone can use their cell phones. Rent should be paid on the 1st of each month, it's late by the 5th, and if they haven't paid by the 15th kick them out. Don't cut your price to help someone out, since the most reliable tenants don't ask for favors.

Manage an Apartment

Become the live-in caretaker of an apartment, and you'll live rent free. You will be expected to perform maintenance duties, and will be on call all of the time. Don't tell anyone you're a student. By the time you get sacked you will have saved at least six weeks' rent.

House Sit

Live in someone else's house, sweep the yard, and keep the place clean in exchange for free board. Your length of stay may vary from a few months to a year, so be flexible and you may even be able to skip from one luxurious house to another.

Take Care of a Boat

If your college town has a waterfront, ask around to find a boat owner who needs a responsible, non-smoking, clean person to stay on board to keep it tidy and vandal-free. You could end up taking care of a huge luxury vessel, docked all year round, and you may only have to vacate it for a few weeks each year. Meanwhile, tell everyone the boat belongs to your parents and then ask the gold-diggers who want to hook up with you to form an orderly line.

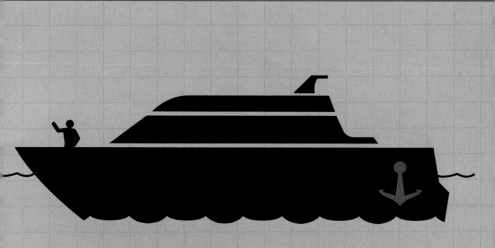

12. Freak Out Your Roommate:

The desensitization of today's youth is a much larger topic than it is possible to cover here. Suffice it to say that these days if you want to screw with your roomie's sanity, hanging your Robert Pattinson poster upside down just won't cut it.

Neurotic Disorder

Vacuum sealed space bags are ideal for transporting clothing to college. Once you've unpacked, use them as dust covers for your PC, bed, pillow, lamp, toothbrush, hamster, etc. Nothing will soil your roommate's khakis quicker than the thought of spending a year living with a clean freak. To complete the look, shuffle around the room wearing a face mask and tissue boxes for slippers muttering, "I wish I could die in my sleep."

Dry Erase Board

Stick a large dry erase board on the back of the door (next to your ankle-length waterproof autopsy apron) so every morning you can leave a freaky message for your roommate ("I can splatter your cortex or explode your heart, which sounds quicker to you?") or to yourself ("Remember to see RA about lactation fetish").

Body Parts and Bedpans

Decorate the walls with your collection of crypt panels, Victorian bedpans, and all your underwear (which "just doesn't get enough oxygen in a drawer"). Keep a diaphonized fetal pig inside your lava lamp and explain that your latest hobby is reducing baby farm animals and road kill to their skeletal frame and then staining them for enhanced bone visibility.

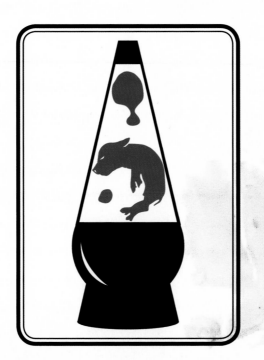

Restraints

Customize your bed with leg irons and wrist shackles. Then apologize: "I wish I could tell you that these are more for my safety than for yours, but I'd be lying . . ." An additional way to spruce up your bed is to embroider the words "I see dead people" onto your pillowcase.

Plush Toys

Don't speak to your roommate directly. Insist that he communicate with you only through your teddy bear, Pennywise the Clown (or any other plush toy inhabited by a shape-shifting, homicidal entity).

Blood Puddle Pillow

Buy a white area rug and a blood puddle pillow (Google it). Every time (and we mean, *every* time) your roomie enters, you should be lying face down bleeding out. To mix things up, hang yourself in the window occasionally too.

Black Out the Windows

Calm your roommate's anxiety by explaining that contrary to their portrayal in B movies and the media, vampires don't need to feast on human blood . . . every night.

13. Sleep with Your Professors:

It's worth considering that professors are older versions of nerds you wouldn't have dreamed of dating in high school. But the power dynamic and the pay check give them an edge, plus the thrill of doing something forbidden. Don't expect to discover anything deeper than a brief spell of mutual gratification.

Wait Until the Grades Are In

It is generally a bad idea to hit on your professors while you are still taking their courses. Most colleges consider this grossly unprofessional and a sackable offense, so the stakes will usually be too high—unless you are really hot and leave them with no doubt about your intentions and your discretion. The best time to hook up is after you get your grade, then no one can say that you traded sex for that A. However, that shouldn't stop you from flirting during the whole semester. Sit up front; wear a short skirt if you're a woman; maintain eye contact during lectures; touch their arm or leg during conversation. You could even lick your lips, or have a wardrobe malfunction (it's hard to misinterpret a nip slip, or a ball sack exposure).

Sexual Harassment

During the '60s, professors and students were all jumping in and out of each other's beds, but in the modern climate of sexual harassment, professors have to be very careful about how they behave. That means that you've got to make your interest very clear. If you are a woman, you will have to make all the moves, rather than drop a few hints and wait for him to move in on you.

Behind Closed Doors

At the end of the course, after the grades are in, make an appointment to see your professor. Tell them how much you enjoyed their course, that you trust and respect their opinion, so you would like help with a personal matter. Ask if you can close their door; if they refuse, then they aren't interested. Say you have a friend who wants to become involved with their professor and doesn't know what to do. If your professor says it's a bad idea, you know where you stand. If they are undecided, then they still need convincing that you are interested and that you won't tell everyone. If they have positive response, suggest a bar somewhere quiet where you can continue your discussion and take it from there.

14. Use Sex to Pay for College:

Selling your body or that of a friend and taking a cut can be an excellent way to fund your college career, especially if you majored in women's studies and plan a career in marriage counseling. It's less time-consuming that waiting tables— you can earn a lot of money quickly, leaving you more time to study. It also gives you a chance to get to know your professors better outside of lecture and seminars.

Auction Your Virginity

If you're hot, auction your virginity online to the highest bidder and bullshit the world about how empowered you feel because you are being "pro-choice" with your body. If you're really lucky you'll get so much free publicity that you won't have to go through with the sordid act. If a one-night-only prostitution package doesn't appeal to you, think of the alternative: a sweaty and unsatisfying five-minute bang with somebody you picked up at the bar when you had your beer goggles on.

Pros: You'll get lots of media attention and be hailed as a brilliant capitalist.

Cons: You'll get lots of media attention and be hailed as an expensive ho.

Pimp Out a Friend

The two things you need to become a pimp, apart from some bitches, is a Cadillac and a gun. No wait, make that two guns—a 9mm to hide in your pocket and something big like an Uzi under your bed for when the turf wars reach your dorm. Pimp your ride with some fur seats, hydraulics, and a CD-auto-changer. Fur coat and bling is optional, although when the bullets start flying, you'll wish you were wearing some dookie rope to bounce some lead.

Pros: You'll never have to hit the streets for sex—your ho should keep you happy.

Cons: Pimpin' ain't as easy as it looks, especially if a hat and cane don't suit you. You'll spend half of your time slapping your bitch up, and the other half being shot at by rival pimps, so squeezing in some lectures may be a challenge.

15. Draw Up a Roommate Contract:

A roommate prenup is a noble enterprise, bursting with good intentions about fair play and mutual respect. But if the contract were honest and sensible, here's what it would really say:

ROOMMATE CONTRACT

We the undersigned enter into this rental agreement for [address] from this [day] of [month], [year]. We are sound of mind, albeit possibly still a bit drunk from last night. We hope we don't lose our deposit, but let's face it dude, we probably will.

This agreement shall remain in effect from [start date] to [end date]. If for any reason a roommate moves out before the date shown (to live with his obsessive leech girlfriend), he will leave everyone else in the financial shit unless a replacement is found. The substitute roommate will be a Psycho Christian Zealot or a Kinky Trailer Park Skitzo on a Welfare Scholarship, but the remaining roommate(s) will approve him/her rather than suffer a rent hike.

The roommates have paid a security deposit of $_____ each, but at the end of the lease they will violently disagree about how many holes they each have kicked in the drywall (which to repair shall cost significantly more than deposit anyway). Besides, our skanky landlord never fixed the hot water boiler all year and we suspect he hid a webcam in the bathroom, so screw him.

Each roommate shall pay $_____ in rent a month, but during the third semester _____ (who we all hate by the way) will suddenly complain how small his room is, even though he lived in it quite happily for the last eight months and will call a house meeting to try to get some of his rent refunded. What an asshole.

Household supplies shall include such things as paper towels, toilet paper, bongs, kegs, cleaning supplies, pregnancy testing kits, duct tape, plastic trash bags, the novelty Osama Bin Laden toilet bowl brush, and any other miscellaneous goods needed for the home which will be shared by ALL roommates.

If two of the roommates build a beer can couch in a communal area, then it shall be the responsibility of the remaining roommates to dispose of the cans at the end of the lease.

All roommates shall pair up and bitch about how they pay for all the food and clean up around here, and that the others don't pull their weight. It will be the responsibility of the roommate deemed to be the most tight-assed to leave terse Post-It notes on the fridge urging other roommates to clean up occasionally—they shall respond by licking all his cheese slices.

Roommates agree to refrain from borrowing others' personal goods, unless they "really needed it" and "thought you wouldn't mind."

Roommates agree to share the responsibilities of cleaning and maintenance of the premises in direct proportion to how much they give a shit about cleaning and maintenance.

In addition to the items aforementioned, roommates agree to argue about:

Keys, cleaning up after parties, parking, quiet hours for studying and sleeping, behavior of guests, taste in music.

Signatures:

_____

_____

_____

_____

16. Get into Secret Societies:

If you're the sort of person who can't enjoy a party for fear of missing out on a better one somewhere else, where the dress code is BMBG ("black mask bring a goat") and the theme is "plotting to bring about a one world government," then getting tapped by a secret society should be high on your to-do list. Shrouded in mystery and usually having more money than morality, these bastions of privilege are independent from the schools where they are located, and many own the buildings where they meet, so the only limit to their "good works" are Hegel's dialectic and the liquidity of the global heroin market.

Do Your Homework

Many secret societies don't even reveal their real names and activities until after you've joined, so make sure you at least get a hint of what the society is about, be it burning kittens to starting forest fires, otherwise you'll join the cool and cryptically named ZZ Top and 77 Society, only to run into fourteen burly seniors wearing fake beards and sombreros tugging on their chorizos and staring fixedly at your Adam's apple. Similarly, before joining the Secret Owl Society, make sure it isn't a worldwide forum for people interested in owls.

Many only admit 15 or 16 in a year, usually from influential families and those of former members. So, if you were born a nobody, you'll have to find another route to world domination.

Ritual

Try to join a society that keeps the ritual to a minimum, because after the novelty has worn off, all those hand gestures and lying naked in a coffin detailing your sexual exploits can become very tiresome.

What's in a Name?

Most of these societies follow the tradition set by Skull and Bones, and have two parts to their name. However, this means that they run the risk of sounding like quaint British biker pubs.

Tapping

On Tap Day stand in the quad with all the other junior hopefuls. If you feel a tap on your shoulder, walk purposefully up to your dorm room and await further instructions. There, in private, you will be given the choice of accepting or rejecting an offer of membership. If you don't feel a tap – don't despair: It may simply be an indication that you're at MIT instead of Yale.

17. Major in Laziness:

Sitting on the couch while work piles up can be tough, but when you procrastinate, enjoy it. Don't sit worrying about your term paper deadline; have another beer instead. This way you won't waste the whole day fretting, and your term paper still won't get written. If you feel guilty, just sit still for five minutes, take several shallow breaths, and reach for another bag of Cheetos. Don't settle for indecision: If necessary, let your self-demotivation take you all the way back to your nice warm bed.

Have a Dream –

Have a dream—a big dream, and if you wake up in the middle of it, go back to sleep and finish it off. Studies have shown that being woken up in the middle of a sleep cycle is very bad for you, so don't get out of bed until you're good and ready.

Have a Hunger –

To be truly demotivated, you need more than a strong urge to stay in bed. You need to be hungry. Your dream can play a big role here too, especially if you dream about being really hungry and wake up craving eight grilled cheese sandwiches. In many cases, hunger makes the difference between skipping breakfast or eating until there's no point in turning up for your first lecture.

Run Your Own Race

The only person you need to beat is you, so relax—how hard can that be? Remember the hare and the tortoise and ignore anyone who tells you that you will only graduate by changing your attitude. Go at your own pace, even if some days you don't make it past the front door. And if you have a hangover, just focus on making it to the couch. Don't think about how many beers you are going to drink this evening—you're bound to feel almost human by then.

Indulge Your Feelings

What stops you working? Are you unmotivated because you are tired, bored, hungry, or hungover? If you don't pin down your feelings, how can you expect to indulge them? There is no simple solution to develop a lack of motivation.

Plan Ahead

While you kick back today, try to imagine how you can waste tomorrow as well. Building momentum early in the day can usually carry you forward far later into an all-night bender, or a George Romero moviethon.

18. Pimp Your Dorm:

A decade of design shows means that everyone is customising their dorms, but if you pick a few choice items you won't have to blow your budget to add some unique touches to your home away from home. So pimp your pad the smart way to express who you think you are or who you want to be.

SlouchBack

This fabric-covered inflatable transforms your bed into a comfortable couch in just thirty seconds. It means you won't have to bunk your beds to fit in a proper couch, and you can have as many couches as you have beds. And like an AeroBed, it's there when you want it; it's gone when you don't. It even has built-in cupholders. Better still, you can become a campus sales rep and earn five percent commission on all sales you make to your friends, so it pays for itself.

LED Projector

Plasma TVs are so last year—they're heavy, expensive, and get damaged easily, so instead, buy an entry-level HD Ready digital projector, which you can plug into your laptop, desktop, or gaming console to create the portable screen size of your choice. You can pick one up for a few hundred dollars, and it will weigh less than a couple pounds, making it easy to transport to and from college, and all around campus.

Octabong Chandelier

No dorm is complete without a multi-person compartmented bonging apparatus capable of delivering a measurable amount of beer and other alcoholic beverages to as many as eight recipients simultaneously. No more arguing about unequal beer-funnel portions. And on the rare occasions when it's not being used, it hangs decoratively from the ceiling.

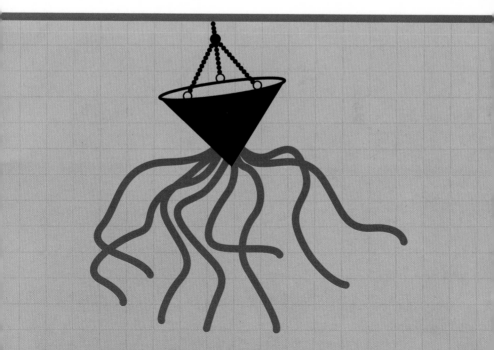

Your Face on Your Bed

You can create your own personalized bedding by soaking your comforter in silver nitrate and then blasting a picture of our face onto it with your HD projector. Use photographic fixative to make the image permanent and if you develop respiratory difficulties, blurred vision, or a burning pain in the throat, see a doctor immediately.

Create the Illusion of Space

Forget shoe organizers, storage tubs, and bed risers: If you don't cut the clutter and keep your space tidy and organized, your tiny room is never going to resemble a loft apartment. Keep walls pictures to a minimum—one large poster or painting works best, so choose carefully. Ramp up your lighting with a 1500-watt halogen bulb—it poses a fire hazard, but brighter rooms look bigger and more welcoming.

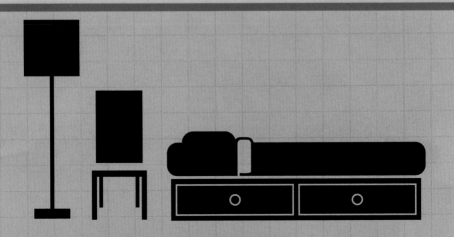

19. Beat the Freshman Fifteen:

We've all heard the scare stories about freshmen gaining fifteen pounds of body fat during their first year at college. Actually studies have shown that it's not as bad as that—the average is between 3 to 10 pounds within the first two years. However, most of this weight is piled on during the first semester of freshman year because of a severe change in lifestyle.

Hall Food

A combination of factors contribute to weight gain. First, while your fruit and vegetable intake will probably decline, you've got a whole world of junk food and high-fat and high-carb hall fodder, snacks, and restaurant portions available, washed down with large quantities of alcohol, which makes you more hungry and leads to late-night snacking, which piles on the pounds. Eat until you are satisfied but not stuffed, and don't use food to line your stomach before a big drinking binge.

Get Plenty of Sleep

Lack of sleep reduces levels of leptin in the body, which leads to an increase in appetite. An irregular sleeping pattern makes it difficult to plan regular meals; if you regularly sleep in late because you were partying until the small hours, it's tempting to skip breakfast and grab a high-carb sugary snack as you run to class.

Exercise Three Times a Week

Unless you join a college team, you will probably exercise a lot less than in high school. Try to build in three 30-minute sessions every week. It doesn't have to be high impact—simply walking briskly to make you out of breath will increase your fitness levels over time.

Stay Hydrated

If you spend every morning hungover, you'll probably spend most of your waking hours feeling dehydrated. Avoid soda; instead, and hydrate by drinking at least eight glasses of water each day, which also helps to reduce hunger and flushes out toxins.

Take a Stress Break

Stress has a major impact on weight gain, from coping with a new environment to study pressures to hectic schedules. Try to find alternative ways to de-stress that don't involve alcohol or drugs, so that you don't spend every evening getting trashed.

20. Get Your Textbooks for Free:

A recent survey estimated that students spend an average of $1,000 a year on books, but you can save large amounts of cash if you know where to look. First off, don't buy every book on the reading list at the start of the semester. Instead, wait until you're going to cover it in class. You may end up not needing all the books the professor originally assigned.

College Library

This seems kind of obvious, but you'd be surprised how many students waste money buying books on their reading list, when there are several copies of the most popular titles in the library. If a book is recommended during a lecture, get to the library as soon as possible and snap it up.

Intercollegiate book sharing networks give you access to hundreds of college libraries for free, but they charge hefty fines for being overdue.

Older Editions

It isn't always necessary to get the latest edition. Publishers constantly make minor changes and republish so they can make more money, so the 91st edition may serve you just as well as the 15th.

Public Domain

Many classics are so old they're in the public domain and can be accessed at one of the many free Web libraries, such as the Internet Public Library, Bartleby, Project Gutenberg, or Googlebooks and GoogleScholar. You can download them to your desktop or a portable device like an iPhone.

Study Group

Form a study group and share the burden of finding books between several people.

Ask Your Professor

If you are desperate your professor may have a spare copy you can borrow, but don't make a habit of it or you'll appear disorganized and dependent.

Open Educational Resources

Groups like Connexions or the Open Educational Resources Consortium are made up of college staff and professors who post textbooks and lessons online. There are also many e-textbooks available. However, many of them can only be read online, their quality isn't that good yet, and they can be expensive.

Book Swapping Websites

Log on to TextbookRevolt.com, Bookins.com, SwapTree.com, or another textbook swapping site and swap your textbooks for free. Currently the choice is limited, but still better than wasting $300 on a new book.

Beyond Amazon

If you can't track down the book you want for free, there are lots of alternatives to Amazon.com, like Half.com (part of eBay) and Alibris.com. Also check CompareTextbook.com before parting with any cash. This site will give you a range of prices across several online bookstores.

21. Treat Your Folks Like an ATM:

It is less morally objection-able to milk as much cash out of your parents now while it can do some good, rather than to sit back and watch them pour it into property and stocks and lose everything in the next economic meltdown. So go on—knock your-self out.

Cashback

If you are paying for tuition and your parents are paying for board, get them to agree to a cashback scheme so for every A you get a refund of 15 percent of your tuition from them. If you take eight classes and get A's in all of them, they'll have to pay for your tuition plus hand over a 20 percent bonus on top. They'll be so proud of your achievements they'll overlook that they are paying you to major in watching porn and *Star Trek* (see page 168).

Avoid the Guilt Trip

Don't get into discussions about how much your parents earn or their spending plan. Tell them you respect their boundaries and that you don't want to know about their finances. The more details they tell you the more they can guilt trip you about spending their hard-earned money.

Short on Necessities

Be specific about why you need the extra money, or they will assume that you simply overspend. Explain that there are several textbooks you need to buy, or that you are skimping on buying necessities like underwear and toothpaste just to balance your budget. Or scare them into treating you to an expensive meal by telling them your microwave broke and you are living on uncooked instant noodles.

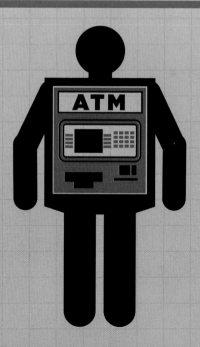

Be Persistent

Don't take NO for an answer. Remember how you used to grind them down every Christmas by whining about the latest video game you wanted? If it worked back then, and if they still love you, it can work again. Point out that if they don't give you more money it shows they don't love you.

Be Grateful

If you want to keep on receiving big time, show your gratitude. Tell your parents that they are the best; this reinforces the connection between good parenting and throwing their cash in your direction.

Stage Your Own Abduction

If none of the above works, then stage your own abduction and get them to send unmarked bills to a prearranged PO Box or public trash can. Cut off one of your fingers and mail it to them with a note saying that you will cut off a whole hand if they call the Feds.

22. Get the Best Seat in Class:

A student's choice of seat has a direct impact on their grades, and also their degree of success in hitting on fellow students. Don't plop yourself down in the first available seat, but consider your options carefully, especially if you want to have the best view of someone else's exam.

Seat Grab

On the first two days of class, sit at the back of the room and check out where the hottest girl is sitting. On the third day, arrive early and sit in her place. When she turns up to find you have stolen her seat, she will be pissed at first, and will slump down in the nearest available seat, right next to you. Then casually look over, introduce yourself and say, "I'm sorry, but I think I may have taken your seat. Would you like to swap places?" Not only have you broken the ice, you'll also make her think you are considerate and sensitive to the feelings of others— plus she gets her favorite seat back and you get to sit nearby and stare at her when she isn't looking.

Center Mass

If academics are your priority, try to sit near the front in the middle of the classroom. As the lecturer talks her eyes will sweep from left to right and up and down, but she will focus the majority of her attention in the center. So long as you are attentive she will get the impression that you are taking a more active part than those sitting at the periphery. If you like goofing off while the lecturer's back is turned, be aware that she is more likely to pick up movement in her peripheral vision, so you should sit at the back center rather than at the sides.

Stay Awake

If you have a problem staying awake, sit next to a window. The natural sunlight will remind your brain that it is daytime and that you should be alert. On the other hand, if you are easily distracted by scantily clad students playing Frisbee on the lawn outside, position yourself as far away from the window as possible. If there are no windows, sit near the front.

Nasty Habits

If you like picking your nose or scratching your ass during lectures, sit at the back. That is the only way to reduce your chances of being seen by everyone else. If you are hungover and think you might puke at any moment, sit by the nearest exit.

23. Survive Rush Week:

Every fall and spring semester, sororities and fraternities have Greek Week or Rush Week, for which they spend all year preparing. Like most institutions, religions, and businesses, they exist solely in order to perpetuate themselves and most of their energies are directed toward this goal. If you want to be part of that nonsense, then you are clearly boardroom material and already understand how this crazy world works.

Enjoy Yourself

If going to invite-only parties and open house parties, or even theme parties isn't fun, maybe Greek life isn't for you. Don't take it too seriously, especially if you don't get into your first-choice fraternity. The intensity of Rush Week can make you forget that the whole world and your place in it does not rest on the outcome of your pledging.

Don't Pledge Freshman Year

You can't really know the character of different fraternities until you've spent a semester or two on campus. Even if your brother or father belonged to a certain one, that doesn't mean it is the same happening place it was when they were there, since frats can change character from year to year. Even if you are a "legacy" (a shoe-in through familial connections), don't race into anything. Greek life will eat up a lot of your time, so choose wisely.

Do Your Research

Make sure you find out about the fraternity, so you know what you're getting into. Some will be for partiers, others for more academic types. Follow your instincts: If something feels wrong, don't do it. Being a self-determined individual with self-respect is better than joining any fraternity.

Flying Alumni

When short on members, some chapters draft in active members from other campuses to attract pledges during Rush Week. Check out last year's group photo to see how many active members there really are on campus.

Hazing

This has all but died out, so there are plenty of fraternities to choose from that won't spend a week humiliating you. Also, most frats are closely regulated by the Pan-Hellenic Council. Whatever happens to you as a pledge, remember that whatever you subject yourself to is still YOUR CHOICE.

24. Haze the Next Pledge Class:

Hazing has earned itself some bad press recently, so many colleges have outlawed and even discontinued the practice. However, it enjoys a rich historical and anthropological pedigree and performs an identical function to any other rite of passage—except that the potential for nudity, sexually oriented humiliation, and serious injury is significantly greater. Pledging is, of course, stupid and pointless, so the hazing stage needs to be sufficiently extreme so that the pledges perceive the process as being very important, and the fraternity as very exclusive. They must feel they are putting themselves on the line, since we are all social creatures with a need to bond. As long as you remember this, there's really no limit to the ways you can mess with their heads. For your peace of mind, the hazing suggestions below have been fully endorsed by Donald Rumsfeld.

Sleep Deprivation

Lack of sleep will enhance any week of hazing. Wake pledges regularly during the night by banging on their doors then make them perform pointless chores, while you play "Barney I Love You" on repeat.

Impossible Tasks

Give the pledges impossible tasks to perform in front of frat brothers who should mock them for their incompetence. These tasks can include eating six saltine crackers in one minute, break dancing while licking their own elbow, trying to stand on their heads while reciting the Greek alphabet, being hung upside-down and slapped until they lose consciousness, and being subjected to electric shocks.

Branding

Blindfold the pledges and inform them they are going to be branded with the fraternity mark. Dunk branding irons in ice water and then press them against a new member's butt cheek. They won't be able to tell the difference between hot and cold, and will think they've been branded with a hot iron, but no harm done—well, not physical, anyway.

Avoid Fragging

Don't go so far beyond the bounds of moral decency that you kill anyone, or worse, become the target of fragging—a practice much used in Vietnam where unpopular senior officers were killed by their own men—like Elias in *Platoon*, only with a fragmentation grenade. As organizer of the hazing, make sure that you deny any knowledge of torture and abuse occurring on campus.

25. Start Your Own Fraternity:

Joining these elite social groups to facilitate wild partying and lots of sex (and if their PR is to be believed, plenty of charitable works) holds a certain attraction (apart from the charity part). Who wouldn't want to gain a band of brothers who will stand by you for life, or simply drag you to the john so you can barf? However, pledging is a big pain in the ass, the dues are expensive, the time commitment is prohibitive, and once you've finished pledging, you'll probably realize you have little in common with most of the other brothers after all. There is a cheaper and more empowering alternative: Start your own.

Decide What You Stand For

Write down about ten goals or ideals to which your organization should aspire. Don't sweat it if you struggle to reach ten—even the Founding Fathers were only able to think of three self-evident truths. Don't worry if most of them are about keggers and getting laid, but remember to add a few worthy aspirations about being an asset to campus life, so when you ask for the Dean's approval you don't look like a members-only boning club.

Name It

Devise a short motto that expresses your philosophy, and then write the initial letters of each word in Greek. Keep it brief because T-shirt logo printers charge by the letter. Some mottos like "Ethanol" or "Θα σου πιω το αίμα" (I will drink your blood) don't need any embellishment.

Collect Your Dues

One of the downsides of belonging to a fraternity is the dues, which can range from $300–$1500 a semester, about half of which goes to the national headquarters. No wonder they want to get pledges. But if you start your own, you ARE the headquarters—you're the top of the whole stinking pyramid. Even if your fraternity is just you and your rich gullible roomie, you get to keep all the money, so long as you spend a nominal amount on ritual props, fake blood, goats, past exam papers, books, banners, and other necessities.

Get Recognition from the Pan-Hellenic Council

After you've taken part in some campus events, approach the Pan-Hellenic council and ask if you can join. Don't worry if they threaten to ban you from campus—bribe them with your first semester's dues and everything you make above that is clear profit.

26. Get Served Underage:

A bar can lose its licence if it is caught letting in or serving underagers, so the stakes are high. Whatever scam you pull to get past security, dress appropriately, look confident, and make good eye contact. Many 18+ clubs draw an X on your hand if you are underage, so before you go out cover your hand with clear glue. This way you can peel off the X in the bathroom. If that won't work, try these tricks before shelling out $100 for a fake ID.

Underage ID

If it's busy, sometimes just holding your underage ID ready and visible is enough to get you waved through.

Smoke Break

Pretend you've already been inside and you stepped out for a smoke or some fresh air—it's lame, but has been known to work.

VIP Status

If someone you're with who is of legal age can get a VIP upgrade (maybe they know the bar owner), there's a chance the bouncers will wave through your whole party without checking everyone's IDs.

Fake Wristbands

Colored wristbands are a common form of age identification in clubs, and they can easily be faked by either buying a set of bands off the Internet, or carrying your own collection of ¾-inch thick paper tape in a variety of colors. The most common colors are neon pink, neon yellow, neon green, neon orange, and white, but you'll also need a range of pastels.

Dragged from Work

Tell the doorman you just finished work and got dragged straight here by your hot boss (it helps if she's over 21), and didn't have time to go home to get your ID.

The Haley Joel Osment Method

If you have a friend who looks really young (about twelve) but is actually twenty-two, he will always get stopped first. The bouncers will spend lots of time scoping his ID, and they will ask lots of questions; after that, if the line is stacking up behind, they will probably wave the rest of you through.

Fake Ticket

It's easy to get served at a ticket-only event. You just need to worry about getting in. You can fake a ticket by scanning a real ticket and printing your own copy. (You can even buy special scissors to cut perforations.) This probably won't work though if the tickets have serial numbers and the bouncers are crossing out names and numbers at the door.

– Use the Dress Code –

Break the dress code so you are refused entry. Explain that you live very close, and can run home to change if they'll let you skip the line when you get back. If the bouncer agrees, it's possible that when you return he'll remember you and let you in without checking your ID.

Hand Stamp

Hand stamps are becoming more sophisticated, and many can only be seen under a black light, but the old-fashioned visible stamps can be faked using a sharpie marker, and then smudging it a bit. Or, you can find someone with a stamp and use a solvent to wet the ink, press their hand against yours, and transfer the mark.

Go Early, Stay Late

Many places only start checking IDs after 9 P.M., so you can go early to joints that serve food, eat, and then stick around as the over-21 crowd arrives.

Passport Scan

Take a color scan of your passport, change your age on Photoshop, print a copy on a high-quality printer, and tell the bouncer you lost your actual passport but the government office sent you a copy of the identification page.

Designated Driver

Explain that you are over 21 but you're not drinking tonight because you're the designated driver for a bunch of friends who are already inside.

27. Throw a Kicking Keg Party:

A keg party is a great way to have all your stuff trashed and/or stolen, get college officials pissed at you, and facilitate the alcohol poisoning of strangers who crash your party. However, with a little planning, your keg party should be memorable, not one people want to forget.

Move Your Stuff to Secure Your Apartment

Lock all bedrooms and bathrooms that you want to keep people out of during the party, and carry the keys with you. Then, clear out the party areas to remove anything valuable or breakable. Also remove anything that could cause an injury or be used as a weapon. Don't be tempted to break your own rules during the party—once you let one couple get jiggy in a previously locked room you open the floodgates for getting your stuff trashed.

Rearrange the furniture to maximize space. If you've got a good carpet, cover it with a plastic tarp for protection. Black out all the windows and keep them shut (and locked, if possible) so you don't disturb the neighbors. Turn down the heating—the place will soon warm up when it's filled with a hundred sweating bodies.

Plenty of Trash Bags

Put a forty-gallon garbage can in every room, lined with a heavy-duty trash bag; if guests can't see a bin nearby you can bet they'll dump their crap on the floor.

Block Off the Kitchen

Put some crates in the doorway and set up a makeshift bar. That way you stop all the alchies from gathering in there and you can cut off the supply if the party starts to get out of control. Make sure you offer your guests plenty of water, so they can keep hydrated.

Sound System

Load up the evening's music on your iPod or computer, and keep it in a locked room so that drunk people don't mess around with it. It also means you can control the volume, because the louder the music the rowdier people get, so uncomfortably loud music is a recipe for brawling and blowing chunks.

Doorman

Have someone manning the door at all times to keep out punks and other troublemakers; choose someone who can not only handle themselves, but can also judge and communicate well with people to reduce the need for physical violence.

Police Radio

Get your hands on a police scanner so you can eavesdrop on their communications. If you get wind of an imminent bust, temporarily lock down your party: music off, no one enters or leaves until it's all clear.

The Keg Is King

Treat your keg or kegs with maximum respect, because if the beer sucks, so will your party. Put the keg in a spot where people will be able to access it easily. Place two sacks of ice in a large plastic tub, then sit the keg on top, pour ice and cold water down the sides, and on top of the keg. Only tap the keg after it has settled and cooled for an hour or two. You won't need to pump immediately after tapping because there will be plenty of carbonization already. People always over pump the keg at parties, and then lose lots of beer in foam. Pump the tap only when the beer flow begins to slow down.

28. Crash a Frat Party:

As a guy, crashing a frat party is a good way to get your ass kicked if you don't know what you're doing. When surrounded by testosterone and alcohol, if you screw up, your evening can quickly turn nasty.

Use Your Connections

If you know some of the frat brothers already, there's a good chance you'll be let in without a problem. But if you can't find your buddies quickly, you'll be thrown out pretty fast.

Be Confident

The Bible says, "ask and you shall receive," but if you ask like a loser you'll get treated like one. So be confident, throw your shoulders back, and announce your presence with confidence, but don't be too brash—show respect, because you are still a crasher. Make sure you know if it's a theme party or not, so you can dress appropriately.

Bring Stuff

It's harder to turn someone away when they come bringing booze, but don't assume it's an automatic in. The doorman may just take your stash and slam the door in your face. The best gift you can bring is lots of ladies. And if you do, make sure you go in first. If you're at the back of the queue of hotties, your face could still become intimate with a closed door. If you are asked to contribute toward another keg, don't make lame excuses, just pay up.

Be Social

Don't sit in a corner nursing a bottle—no one needs a bum taking up space. Talk with as many of the brothers as you can, and express an interest in rushing next semester (even if it's not true), and say hello to anyone who makes eye contact otherwise you'll seem hostile. Never hit on anybody's date—guys can get really territorial on their home turf.

Stay in Control

Getting belligerently drunk has three bad results: It draws unwanted attention to you; it makes you less able to handle yourself if things get out of hand; it kind of abuses the hospitality of those who let you in. So watch how much of the free booze you drink. Take part in any drinking games, but don't make a big deal of winning, and don't put others down.

29. Steal Stuff from the Dining Hall:

Each year thousands of items are stolen from college dining halls nationwide, and the cost of replacing them is passed onto the students. You may justify dining hall theft to yourself because you have a high metabolism, or you don't enjoy the luxury of having rich parents to stock your fridge. But you don't need to make excuses because everybody is stealing, and anything that reflects the will of the people is a good thing. In fact, if you don't steal, you actually weaken democracy. Also, when you pay eight dollars for a meal you should get your fair share of utensils and salt shakers, otherwise the dining hall is really stealing from you.

Demand Silverware

It is impossible to steal silverware and quality utensils if they have been replaced by plastic products. If this happens at your college, stand up for your silverware rights and refuse to use plastic cups and utensils just because so many students have been pilfering the regular silverware. You pay enough to eat here, so you should have decent utensils to steal. Robbing the dining hall isn't really stealing if you leave with the intention of returning your plunder at some unspecified time (whether you actually do or not—crime is all about intention).

Backpack and Tupperware

Tupperware is the container of choice for the experienced food thief, but your backpack design is also crucial. Choose one with several outer compartments where you can stash long watertight containers to harvest all sorts of liquids (especially milk). Dry foods such as cereals or self-contained items such as fruit are easy to come by, but don't be discouraged by messier targets such as lasagne, which taste great cold. In fact, the only limit to your creativity should be the size of your backpack and your dreams. How will you ever know if the waffle iron and toaster fit if you don't try?

Manage Your Risk

Your backpack-to-plate ratio should be no greater than 20:1. This means that for every slice of pizza you consume, no fewer than twenty slices should make it back to your dorm.

30. Boot and Rally:

When you've already enjoyed a major bingefest and there are several pressing engagements on your evening's hectic social calendar, sometimes pulling a boot and rally is the sensible choice. Endorphins are released during vomiting so it feels great too! The alternative may be alcohol poisoning, which can lead to coma, brain damage, or death. Don't make a habit of this though because regular puking eats away at tooth enamel and weakens the cardiac sphincter muscle leading to gastric reflux, which screws up your esophagus causing life threatening ulceration and perforation. So remember boys and girls—always toss your cookies responsibly.

The Finger Method

Assume the position—lean forward with your head facing down. Trigger your gag reflex by pressing your middle and index fingers onto the back of your tongue and wiggle them to tickle the back of your throat. This will make you gag and cough; keep going until your stomach starts heaving. Open your throat as if you were is about to swallow a sword; this sends another signal to your brain that a pavement pizza about to be delivered. You should puke in about two minutes max.

Syrup of Ipecac

This poisoning remedy will have you dribbling on the carpet before you can say Ralph Lauren. You can find it in most first aid kits or at your local drugstore. Take two tablespoons of Ipecac immediately followed by three glasses of water. If you haven't blown your chunks after thirty minutes, take one one more dose and no more.

Mustard and Salt

Dissolve three teaspoons of salt in half a liter of hot water followed by 5 ounces of yellow mustard. Drink down in one gulp and then stand back . . . from everything.

2 Girls 1 Cup

If you mistrust emetics and prefer a more organic barfing experience and you have access to the Internet, type "2 Girls 1 Cup video" into a search engine and enjoy this viral barf-inducer, or check out the dead bodies on Rotten.com.

Stress Vomit

Situations of extreme stress causes the body to go into shock, whereupon it eliminates the stomach contents so that it can focus its resources (i.e. blood flow) on dealing with the crisis. So if your drinking buddy is too squeamish to sample any of the above methods, just kick him hard in the nuts.

— 31. Put a Horse in the Dean's Office:

There's an old saying that you can lead a horse to water, but only if you know how to lead a horse in the first place. You can't just tug on its reins and expect it to follow. If a horse is stubborn, the harder you pull, the more resistant it will become. It's not as easy as John Belushi made it appear. For safety, wear a riding helmet and gloves, and leave your starting pistol in your dorm.

Halter the Horse –

Before you can lead a horse anywhere, you must halter it. Unbuckle the halter and hold it in your left hand with the nosepiece dangling beneath. Standing to the left of the horse's right shoulder, throw your right arm around its neck. Grab the right strap of the halter with your right hand, and keep holding the left strap in your left hand. Guide the nosepiece over the horse's muzzle, then tighten the strap over its face and do up the buckles. Attach a strong lead rope to the tie ring underneath the halter.

Hold the Rope

Stand at the horse's left shoulder holding the lead rope in your right hand about eight inches from the snap and the folded end of the rope in your left hand. Make sure that the rope doesn't loop around either of your hands, otherwise you won't be able to let go if the horse bolts.

Cue the Horse to Walk

Cue the horse to walk by bringing your right hand forward, but don't tug or pull. Say "walk" or "come" or whatever word the horse is used to. Start walking forward yourself. When you want the horse to stop, say "whoa" as you stop yourself and pull slightly on the lead rope. Stay calm and relaxed, otherwise the horse will sense your nervousness and become agitated.

Lead the horse into the Dean's office. Close the door and scamper. Hilarity will ensue.

32. Blow Off Your Folks:

If your parents show an unhealthy interest in your college career, making you feel you have to check in three times a week to avoid a guilt-ridden account of their mundane existences, here are a few ways to reduce the time wasted on the phone with your folks.

Heavy Talk

Your parents are happiest when you find something trivial to talk about on the phone, like how your team did at the track meet, or what you had for lunch. This lets them pretend to be interested, and ask you if you're eating enough. So give them the exact opposite—phone every day to lament how bummed out you feel. At first they'll be sympathetic, but after a couple weeks they'll be glad when the calls become less frequent.

Homesickness

Fake homesickness. Tell them that you are miserable and want to quit college and move back with them. This will scare them silly; they just got rid of you—they don't want you back already. Explain that you find it too emotionally draining to call, so you're going to cut back your calls to once a month, to focus on making some kind of life there at college.

Ask for Money

Ask for money every time you talk, and slip hints into the conversation to imply you've developed a drug habit. Soon they'll be glad when your calls become less frequent because they'll think you're getting your life back under control (either that or you've gone into rehab).

Screw with Their TV Schedule

Call when you know that your mom is watching her favorite television show. She'll offer to call you back, and you can make sure you're out when she does. That way you looked willing to talk, but actually didn't' have to spend any time on the phone.

Multitask

Multitask: Only call your folks while you're doing something else—walking to class, riding on the bus, doing your laundry, taking a dump—so you don't waste quality time.

Hang Up

Hang up while you are speaking so they think you were cut off. Leave your phone off the hook so they can't call back—they'll assume you're calling them. Eventually they'll think there's something wrong with your cell reception and give up.

33. Get Away with Being Late to Class:

Being late to class isn't something to be ashamed of—despite the poisonous looks from your professor as you slip quietly into the back of his lecture. It is a sign that you have an active social life. However, you'd better arm yourself with some plausible excuses otherwise your academic reputation will soon be down the toilet. You can place the blame on one of three things: someone else, something else, or yourself.

Blame Someone Else

It's natural and honest to try to shift the blame onto someone else, but the best of these excuses should also make you look good:

"My roommate had a seizure, so I had to wait with him until the paramedics arrived."

"My roommate fell down a mountain and I was the only person qualified to fly the rescue helicopter."

"A group of students were making disparaging remarks about you, so I had to fight them."

Blame Something Else

Inanimate objects make excellent excuse material because most professors will appreciate that entropy in a chaotic universe makes you a hapless victim of events completely out of your control.

"My alarm clock went back to sleep. I didn't want to wake it up."

"The dog ate my car keys and so I had to hitchhike to the vet."

"My lever arch file broke, and the wind blew my papers everywhere, and then a bird flew into my head."

Blame Yourself

Taking responsibility rarely earns you bonus points and can easily backfire, so only use this strategy as a last resort.

"I was at the bank getting another extension on my loan."

"I got delayed by a really bad accident on the freeway that I caused."

"Please punish me. I have been naughty—so very naughty."

The Laws of Blame

1. Keep your excuse simple and to the point; elaboration = fabrication.

2. Only use medical excuses if you have the knowledge to back it up.

3. Blame yourself only if you can't blame someone else.

End Game

Terminal illnesses, deaths in the family, and impromptu funerals have the advantage of being difficult to challenge. If you involve the death of pets, stick to cute furry animals, not dumb, ugly ones like goldfish and iguanas.

34. Take Your Friend's Room Apart in Fifteen Minutes:

You can't call someone a true friend until you've trashed their room and then stood in the corridor cackling like a baboon while he opens his door (assuming you haven't superglued the lock). He gets mad, swears about getting even, and possibly even bursts into tears at the hours of redecorating that lie ahead. If he takes it all in good humor, you have failed, and if he comes back while you're stripping his room, everyone loses. So, with a little planning, you should be able to complete the whole operation in fifteen minutes.

Tooled-up Buddies

A medium-sized single dorm room can be packed with a surprising volume of stuff, so recruit at least nine of your victim's "friends" to make sure the process is slick and swift. Everyone should bring a pair of gloves, a power screwdriver, a claw hammer, and a roll of heavy-duty garbage bags. Divide the team into seven packers and three removers, so the majority of you stay in the room to pack and dismantle, while the other three run around hiding his stuff in other rooms. Only when all the packing has been completed should the packers become removers.

Order of Removal

1. Clear out anything that is immediately visible; all of his stuff that's hanging up, or on his desk, or in his shelves; make sure to snatch anything hanging on the back of the door as well as the posters on the walls.

2. Be smart about how you go about clearing out his things. For example, if the CDs are kept in a portable tower, remove the whole tower, but if the rack is attached to the wall, remove them before you unscrew it. Place screws in small cellophane bag and tape to the relevant items of furniture.

3. Open cupboards and wardrobes, and remove all items.

4. Remove all items of furniture (dismantle as required).

5. Remove duvet and mattress; dismantle and remove the bed.

35. Get the Most Out of Class:

The best way to take notes is when the owner isn't looking. But if you can't steal someone else's notes or there is an attendance requirement for your lectures, these listening techniques will get you through.

Before the Lecture

Make out noisily with your girlfriend. Your body produces pheromones and lots of other feel-good chemicals that will put your brain into a receptive state. Keep sucking face until your lecturer asks you to leave.

iPod

Listening to thrash metal on your iPod may aid the concentration as well as the concentration of those around you. Download an entire season of *The Big Bang Theory*, and watch it during science lectures, to learn about quantum physics.

Be Open Minded

Be open minded to whatever the lecturer is saying; you don't have to agree with it. You can even laugh, shake your head, or sneeze "bullshit" sporadically. At the end of the lecture, ask pointless questions that show you haven't been listening.

Lean Back

Over-eager students often lean forward, which is wrong and makes you look like a pathetic nerd. Write down the title of the lecture and the date, then put down your pen and sit back with your arms behind your head. This funnels the sound into your ears so you don't have to strain to hear.

Stationery

Doodles are the windows to your soul and make the brain more receptive, so have fun and explore your creative side. Have extra pencils sharpened and lots of rolled up chewed paper in case a spitball fight breaks out while the lecturer is writing on the whiteboard.

Passive Listening

One of the study techniques you often hear casually tossed around is "Active Listening." This is nerdspeak for staying awake, and is no fun at all. The top form of listening is "Passive" and it's what you do when you watch your favorite sitcom. Consider how easily you can lose an entire evening vegging in front of the TV without busting a cranial sweat.

Now consider how long you can stay awake in a boring lecture. Clearly passive listening is the only way to prevent burn out and ear infections.

Keywords

If the time is really dragging, count how many times the lecturer uses words like "the" or "a," or flick the ears of the hot chick in front of you every time he makes a lame joke. Listen carefully for keywords and phrases like "finally" and "in conclusion." This is your cue to pack up your stuff so you can be the first out the door as soon as the lecture finishes.

36. Stay Awake During a Lecture:

Staying awake during a lecture may sound a little crazy, since it's probably the only chance you get to catch up on your sleep. However, if you're going to bother to turn up to class you may as well benefit from the experience.

Catch Some Extra Zs

Go to bed an hour earlier (it's boring, and if you live in a dorm or have a nocturnal roommate, it may be impossible). Stop drinking an hour before you go to bed, giving your body more time to process the alcohol, so it isn't working hard when it should be resting.

Take Notes by Hand

Somehow writing is a more active process than dicking around on a laptop, plus you won't be tempted to start IMing your friends or checking your email. If you really can't focus on what the lecturer is saying, then at least keep your eyelids open by keeping a tally of his nervous ticks or the number of times he repeats his favorite catchphrase.

Snack Attack

Don't allow yourself to get hungry. If you feel your energy levels slipping it's already too late, so power up with energizing snacks to keep your blood sugar levels stable, which is especially useful if you went on a bender the night before. More important than eating food is staying hydrated, so take a bottle of water to class. Eat protein at lunch instead of empty carbs like sandwiches and French fries.

Four O'clock Fade

Studies have shown that four o'clock in the afternoon is the worst time for fatigue to sneak up on you. Take a brisk walk for five minutes before the lecture, and then as you sit waiting for the class to begin, take some deep breaths in through your nose, hold it in for a few seconds, and then breathe out slowly through your mouth. This gets the oxygen flowing around your body and clears your fuzzy brain. Sunshine is also a good way to tell your brain to stay awake; even fifteen minutes of rays will make you more perky.

Power Nap

Taking a ten-minute power nap after lunch can keep you going for the rest of the afternoon. However, be warned that dozing for any longer will leave you feeling terrible, and may affect your nighttime sleep pattern.

Essential Oils

Smells are great for busting through the sleep barrier, especially rosemary, peppermint, and orange peel. Keep a small bottle in your pocket and take a good sniff when you feel your spirits sagging.

37. Get Revenge on Your Roommate:

"'Vengeance is mine, I shall repay.' Says the Lord." But why should he have all the fun? When it's time to teach your roommate a lesson, settling the score is always better than talking trash behind someone's back. If you are passive aggressive, anonymous retribution is the way to go.

Mail Bug

The best revenge is when a little initial effort yields lasting results. This is the ultimate long-play revenge prank. Find where he keeps his stash of postage stamps and then use a cotton swab to dab a drop of toilet water onto the back of each one. Each time he mails a letter he'll spend the next day in bed with stomach cramps.

Shirty Tricks

Get a pen that only shows up under a black light. Write "Kick me, I'm a douche bag" on the back of his favorite shirt. Next time he goes clubbing he'll wonder why he is attracting the wrong kind of attention.

Orange Pee

Go to the drugstore and buy some Azo-standard pills. Crush them into a fine powder and then slip them into his drink. They are non-toxic and are used to treat symptoms of urinary tract infections. The next time he visits the bathroom his pee will be orange and he'll think he's got an STD.

Dump in the Closet

Take a dump in a plastic cup and leave it in the bottom of his closet. Next, tear out the last five pages of the book your roommate is reading and leave a note saying that the pages are hidden in the closet.

Library Pervert

Replace your roomie's Windows startup sound with porno sound effects, so that when he boots up in the library everyone thinks he's a perv. Go to the Control Panel, click on the Sounds and Audio Devices tab, and then click on the sound files you want to change. Click "Browse" to find your replacement porno sound (which you have already saved somewhere on his laptop). Now click "Save As" to name your new sound scheme. Select this sound scheme, click "Apply," and exit.

38. Sabotage Your Hall's Bathroom:

The most fun-loving and dynamic students distinguish themselves early in the first semester by their aptitude for sabotaging the hall bathroom. If you have unresolved potty training issues and feel compelled to claim your place as a menace to campus society, here are some ideas.

Beef Shower

There can't be many people left in the Western world that haven't heard of or experienced first-hand the classic bouillon cube shower, but it is rarely used any more, a victim of its own notoriety. Simply unscrew the shower head and place a few bouillon cubes inside. Whoever takes a shower will get covered in meaty goodness, and the more they try to shower away the smell, the worse it will get.

Soap Seal

Coat a bar of soap with several layers of clear nail polish, allowing each coat to dry before applying the next. When the last coat is dry, swap it with a hallmate's bar. Your victim will work themselves into a frenzy trying to wash and they will be foaming at the mouth before the soap produces any lather. You can use the same technique to disable a deodorant stick.

Bubble Flush

Lift the lid off the top of the tank and add a small amount of bubble bath or liquid detergent. The next person who flushes will get an effervescent surprise.

Gelatin Turd

Pour several packets of clear gelatin in the toilet bowl, and stir to dissolve. Then pull down your pants and crank out a large, smelly log. Put an "Out of Order" sign on the stall door, so the gelatin can set for a few days. If you want immediate results, use anhydrous sodium poly-acrylate (available at magic stores) which can hold up to 300 times its weight in water.

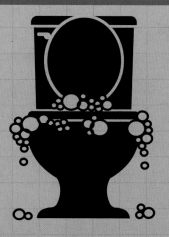

39. Get Someone Strip Searched in the Library:

Watching someone getting strip searched in the college library and knowing that you made it possible has to be the most fun anyone can have in the library.

Magnetic Strips

Most library books have magnetically charged security strips hidden inside; these are made of either iron or cobalt and their polarity is determined by whether or not the strips have passed through a sensitizing/desensitizing machine. The books are sensitized before being shelved. The security gates at the entrance and exit are activated when they detect an active strip. Anyone wishing to take a book through the security gates must first take it to the librarian who will desensitize the strip to reverse the polarity.

To get someone strip searched you must locate one or more strips, remove them from their books, and then hide them in your victim's clothes. Some strips will still set off the detectors even when they have been chopped into small pieces, making them much easier for you to hide and much harder for the security guards to find and remove.

Collect Strips

Depending on their design, the strips can usually be found in one of three places. For a hardcover, open the book as wide as it will go and look between the spine and the binding, then pry away the self-adhesive strip with a knife. Paperbacks and magazines can be protected with an ultra thin double-sided adhesive strip inserted deep in the gutter (the space between the printed area and binding) between two pages rather than in the spine. These are very difficult to spot and even harder to remove without causing damage. And sometimes the strips are clearly visible inside the back cover. Though occasionally, the magnetic sensors aren't strips at all—some are small black circles, or a white square with circuitry underneath.

Set the Trap

Once you have collected several strips, hide them in your victim's clothing (under a lapel, in a skirt or pants hem, inside shoes), their bag or purse, or even their hair (if their hair is messy and thick, or they wear a headband or hat). If you really want to give them trouble, throw a few library books in their bag. Finally, find yourself a comfortable chair and enjoy the show at a safe distance.

40. Make Your Hallway Think You're Having Lots of Sex:

You're not a looker, you don't have much money, and you're not a musician, so how can you convince the guys on your

hallway that you're having lots of sex? First, why not try having sex? Go talk to girls. Also, if you can smell your pits, you need a shower. If you can't smell your pits, you still need a shower. Shower every day. Not only will this improve your chances of scoring outside your own imagination, it will prepare you in case things work out after following the techniques below. Once word spreads that you bed a different girl every night, your social status will improve, and the illusion should quickly become reality.

Invent a Nickname

Insert a "9" between your first and last names. Explain that everyone has used this nickname since sixth grade (even your teachers . . . and your parents) and it kind of stuck. Its ambiguity is its strength: truth or irony? Does it refer to length, frequency, or girth?

Get Busted Busting a Nut

The best way to fool everyone on your hallway that you're having lots of sex is to have sex in the actual hallway. Not all the time though—getting caught grinding with a hot date by the RA during Parents' Weekend will be enough to cement your reputation as the campus stud.

Spread the Good News

Head up a Bible study group. When the guys on your hallway see a parade of chicks wearing promise rings filing in and out of your room, they'll reach one conclusion: you're getting lots of oral, because Jesus says that doesn't count.

That Morning After Feeling

You know that glow you get when you've spent all night having great sex—people notice it, they remark that you're hollow-eyed but kind of smug. You can fake this by staying up playing *World of Warcraft* until 5 A.M. then limping into breakfast after rubbing one out in the john.

Low-Sugar Rush

Make a big deal about stealing "girl food" at breakfast to take back to your room—half a grapefruit, sugar-free frozen yogurt, anything dull and fat free. No time for small talk with the sex-starved losers at your table because you've got a hungry hottie upstairs expecting room service.

41. Find a Campus Booty Call:

When you've been painting the town red but can't persuade anyone to come home to help soak your brushes, a booty call is the perfect standby. However, lining up a sort-of-friend who will respond to impromptu requests for sexual favors requires a certain degree of skill, someone whose desire for mutual gratification outside a traditional relationship with no strings attached is not precluded by their resemblance to a sack of armpits.

Rough Trade Off

The booty call is inevitably a compromise between what you desire and what you'll settle for at the end of an evening: too easy and they'll already be grinding their coffee with someone else; too innocent and you'll wake them up; too ugly and they will have been chased into the hills by a pitchfork and torch bearing mob. Your ideal booty should be homely with low self-esteem, and if you're really lucky—no gag reflex or teeth; preferring to stay in, but likely to be awake in the small hours (studying). We're talking here of course about the honor roll student: after years of failing to live up to ridiculously high parental expectations, in college they rebel by filling the emotional void with a succession of meaningless physical encounters. Remember to utter the phrase "I'm proud of you" as you cum over her tits.

Off-Peak

Avoid booty calling at 3 A.M. on a Friday or Saturday—that's peak-time when everyone is doing it. Don't neglect the other five nights of the week, especially Mondays and Tuesdays when there's less competition or expectation that you'll be drunk and desperate.

Booty Grazing

When your tame honor roll student is unavailable there's nothing to stop you playing the numbers with some "booty grazing." Who says that a booty call has to be a call—it can be a text. Fire off a generic booty text to everyone in your address book you soberly marked with a "Y" (those are the ones you won't regret waking up with tomorrow); if none of them text you back, send one out to all those with an "X" beside their names (ugly in the morning); and only if they don't text you back do you resort to those tagged with a doodle of a skull and bones dissolving in a barrel of toxic waste (ugly all the time).

42. Give Your RA a Nervous Breakdown:

Your resident adviser is a facilitator, rule enforcer, resource provider, subtle encourager of community spirit, handler of emergencies, someone you can speak to about a problem, but most of all they deserve to be the primary focus of your floor's incessant prankage. With collective effort, you should be able to get your RA sacked or to quit within the first semester.

Memory Tricks —

Most RAs pride themselves on getting to know the names of the students—it's the first requirement of the job—so make sure that you answer to a different name every time you see him. Also, if he uses a memory system like flashcards or a photo cheat sheet, screw with it—change the names around, draw in facial hair, use your imagination.

Community Building

A savvy RA won't call a mandatory floor meeting; instead he'll put the word out that the college has given him some money for pizza and that everyone's invited. However, it's your job to taint those pizzas with whatever you can steal from the lab to give everyone food poisoning. He won't be so popular after that. Find out where he keeps his bagels, so when he brings them out every now and then on a Sunday afternoon, you can spike those with some super toxins as well.

Go Over His Head

If you have a problem, always go above your RA's head directly to the Residence Director or the Area Coordinator. They will be annoyed to be disturbed, but it will also make the RA look unapproachable, and that he sucks at his job. After ten students do the same thing, questions will be asked. In confidence, confess that he plays loud music during quiet time, boasts about his free room and board, and regularly sits playing X-Box in the nude with his door open.

Dress This Way

Your RA should be a role model, so much in fact that you and several of your friends want to copy him. Do your hair the same way. Compliment his clothes and ask where they are from. Buy them, wear them, ask him if he'll be your new daddy. Borrow his stuff and spend all your free time hanging out in his room (have everyone else do the same) until he has to kick you out just to get some sleep.

43. Fake a Computer Virus with Your BlackBerry:

This little hi-tech prank will fool your roommate into thinking he has a virus on his PC that announces its presence with infected audio files.

Disconnect PC Speakers

Disconnect the speakers from the PC and connect them to your Bluetooth puck (it's small anyway, but strap it out of sight underneath his desk); now you will be able to send audio messages or music to his speakers and he'll think it's coming from his computer. Make sure the puck is switched on.

Pair Your BlackBerry to Your Puck

Hook up the puck to your BlackBerry and test the connection by streaming an audio file over the PC speakers.

Record a Message

Get a friend (preferably one your victim doesn't know) to provide the voice for an audio file. It should say something like "Hey. You. Yes, you. I've infected your PC with this neat backdoor Trojan. If you run a virus check I'll erase your hard drive." Or "You picked up this trojan on a porn site. Right now I'm sending a screen shot of the last page you visited to everyone on your address list."

Save the file onto your BlackBerry, and then stream it at your will. You don't even have to be in the same room, as you should be able to get Bluetooth coverage from at least 25 feet away.

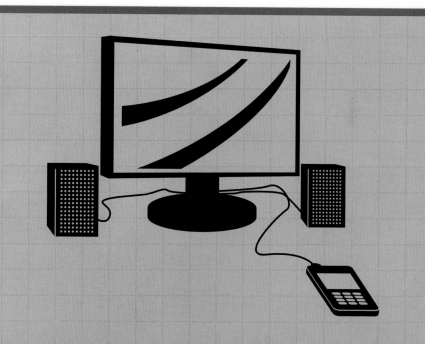

44. Cheat Your Way Through Exams:

When cheating during an exam, apart from not getting caught, prior preparation is vital, as well as an ability to stay calm under pressure when a professor is standing two feet away staring hard in your direction. Stay calm, don't look around, and focus on your work.

Smartphone

A recent Common Sense Media poll found that more than half of teens in the US use smartphones and the Internet to cheat at schoolwork and exams. It concluded: "The unintended consequence of these versatile technologies is that they've made cheating easier." No shit. But why stop there? You can use your phone to send answers to friends who are set to take the same test later that day, as well as exchange texts during the exam. Remember to disable keypad tones and put your phone on silent.

iPod

Use your PC to edit the lyrics boxes in your iTunes library, filling them with the dates, facts, and formulas you need for your exam. Then sync your iPod to download the songs, and access the cheat sheets in the exam by listening to the song and then clicking on the center button until the information appears.

Adhesive Tape

Type the cheat information in four-line paragraphs of Arial, font size 8. This is easy to read, but small enough to cram in lots of data. Print out your notes using a toner-based laser printer at maximum resolution. Stick clear adhesive tape over each paragraph, cut out the strips, and then soak them in cold water for a few minutes until the paper peels away easily. The text should now appear on the tape. Stick the tape where necessary (up your arm, on the inside of your thigh, your pen, under your hoodie, inside your belt, inside a charity or friendship bracelet, etc.).

Food and Drink

Anything that contains a label can be customized either on Photoshop or using the adhesive tape method to replace or supplement the nutritional information with cheat data. If you can read Japanese, Korean, or Chinese (or failing that, any foreign language), write your cheat data in one of these languages and even under close inspection it will look authentic.

Friendship Bracelet

Use a set of felt tip pens to decorate a friendship bracelet with a color-coded sequence. This can be used to record the answers to a multiple choice exam, so long as you have already managed to steal the answer sheet, or buy the answers from an older student. A=Black, B=Yellow, C=Red, and so on, depending on how many answer choices there are.

Rubber Band

Take one thick runner band and stretch it to its limit between two nails. Write your information on the band with a black ballpoint pen. Release the tension and the words will shrink to illegible marks, until you are ready to stretch the band (or "bracelet" as it has now become) in the exam to reveal your hidden message.

Hidden Earpiece

A Canadian company called ExamEar offers a range of tiny wireless earpieces and microphones with the slogan "helping students succeed." They can easily be used to communicate with someone outside the exam, but hurry up and buy one before the company gets closed down. If so, look for similar gadgets on amateur spying and espionage websites.

45. Survive Your First Christmas Vacation:

After the excitement of your first semester at college, returning home for the Christmas vacation can be a tough and confusing gig—becoming a child again, living by your parents' rules, maybe holding down a mindless and repetitive job with a bunch of hicks you thought you'd escaped forever by going to college, all the while counting the days until the start of the new semester.

This Too Shall Pass

They may seem like the longest four weeks of your life, but as sure as the Antarctic ice sheet is growing, you'll be back with your real friends before too long. Avoid clock watching; in fact, lock your wristwatch in a drawer, unplug your alarm clock, and close your curtains so you won't be tempted to divide the sky into twelve imaginary sections of one hour each and then plot the path of the sun or moon across it. Lie on your bed, curl into a ball, and hug your knees, but don't count your heartbeats or tune into the blood pumping through your temples to keep track of time. Try to get some sleep and look on the bright side: so far no one has actually used those dreaded words "curfew" and "not while you're living under my roof," you've only been sent to your room twice, and you get a yummy cookie whenever you go potty.

Show Them You Are Responsible

If you really cannot stand being treated like a child, you need to demonstrate to your parents that their little baby is grown up in terms they can understand. You know that you're officially an adult now, but they won't appreciate that you've recently lost your virginity and discovered that you can funnel six beers without puking. So sip your drinks slowly, wear a sweater, develop an interest in cholesterol-lowering yogurts, watch cable news with the sound up loud, enjoy long walks, and don't leave the house without an umbrella.

Renew Old Ties

So you don't get blown off by your friends back home, fire off a few emails before you leave college, otherwise you've only got yourself to blame if all your buddies make plans that don't involve you. Don't be surprised if while you've been away blowing your parents' money on an education, they too have moved on with their lives—some will be pregnant, others in prison, and the rest can be found tasering motorists for minor traffic violations.

46. Get a College Loan with Bad Credit:

If your credit rating is less than satisfactory, you might think that nobody will lend you any money, but there are actually lots of financial institutions that will throw good money after bad. Even post credit crunch they haven't learned their lesson, which is great for you.

Check Your Credit Report

Don't accept what you've been told—check it out for yourself by subscribing to one of the online credit report agencies, which will show you where it all went wrong and what you defaulted on in the past. Check the accuracy of the report because it may be out of date, leaving you in the clear to get into more debt.

Pawn Shop Loan

That Rolex your parents gave you for your eighteenth birthday will look just fine on the shelf of the local pawn shop. No identification required, and no credit check. Just hand over the item for valuation and you will be offered a percentage of its value, and then a ticket which allows you to reclaim the item by paying back the loan plus interest within a few months, or extend the loan by just paying the interest.

Use Collateral

A secured loan requires the borrower to pledge some asset (a car or property) as collateral for the loan. You probably don't have much collateral, apart from your iPod, some CDs, and an empty keg, but who has a house and car that you know? Get your parents to secure your loan against their house. They'll think this means that you'll be extra responsible about paying it back, since you wouldn't want them to have to sell their house, but what it really means is that even if you default on the loan, your parents will have to bail you out so they don't get evicted. You can't lose.

Improve Your Credit Rating

Thinking longer term, you can improve your credit rating by showing that you can be trusted with a small amount of credit. For example, if your credit rating is so bad you can't even get a small loan, you may still be able to get a "credit card for people with bad credit." The advantage is that you don't have to pay off a fixed amount each month, and you may be able to get an introductory interest-free period. Mainstream lenders won't touch you, but once you have your crappy little card with a small lender, you can improve your credit rating by using your card a little each month and paying it off reliably. Within a year you can dramatically improve your credit score, overturn your bad rating, and then take out another card or a loan with a higher borrowing facility.

47. Pretend to Be a Visiting Professor:

Posing as a visiting professor is one of the most cost effective ways of enjoying college life, since the faculty will pay you for your dubious contribution to academic excellence and be so relieved to have hired a workhorse without tenure that they'll pretty much leave you alone to work the students to death. Bank your grant in an unnumbered Swiss account, play the system, and they won't be able to claw back the money once your cover is blown.

Be Foreign

You are on sabbatical from another really good school, but don't choose an American college for your back story, as it is easy for anyone to call them or check your existence and credentials online. If you don't show up on the list of staff, you'll be found out before you've managed to tuck into your first plate of veal and truffles in the professor's dining room. Instead, pick a non-English speaking country that isn't easily traceable, somewhere in the former Eastern Bloc or Africa, with a language with which few students will be familiar, so they can't find you out by conversing in your so-called mother tongue. If you are worried about getting found out, set up a fake website for your made-up college and post your fake resume there.

Choose a Bullshit Specialty

You probably don't know much about very much, so it's best to play it safe and say that back home you are a professor from the Department of Earth and Environmental Sciences. Then if anyone challenges your credentials you can deflect attention by bursting into tears and carrying on about land subsidence, inflow of seawater in local rivers during high tide, and how your beloved country will be under three feet of water within ten years. Begin every other sentence with "In my country . . ." and make frequent comments about the size of restaurant portions and how much you are enjoying visiting a vast-consuming empire and miss eating curried dog.

Act Crazy

Visiting professors are always crazy and demanding workaholics who expect their students not to have lives outside of studying either. They have lots of energy and enthusiasm for their subject but often little to no experience of teaching, so don't give the game away by being either a good communicator or delivering an interesting or relevant lecture.

48. Fund Your Way Through College with a Dotcom:

The best thing about the Internet isn't the porn, or the streaming movies, or social networking, or shopping, it's that the potential to make enormous sums of money never diminishes, and unlike many other fields, it isn't a zero-sum game. People all over the planet are becoming millionaires with new ideas. Within a few months you too can be making so much money you won't bother going to college.

- Milliondollarhomepage.com -

One of the simplest and most successful dotcoms was a single webpage. On August 26, 2005 twenty-one-year-old Alex Tew from Wiltshire, England launched *www.milliondollarhomepage.com*. He aimed to make a million dollars by selling advertising—1,000,000 pixels for $1 each. Within five months he made a gross total of $1,037,100.

Write a Blog -

If Perez Hilton and John Chow (took his blog from zero to $40,000 dollars a month within two years) can do it, why not you? First you need to register a domain name and find a cheap web host. Then load a blogging platform like WordPress onto your server (it's free) and start blogging away. Either write about stuff that interests you, or research keywords to find out what people are searching for online, and then write about that. Then bone up on search engine optimization, pepper your blog with Google AdSense ads, affiliate links, and pay-per-click advertising, and sit back and watch your income streams burst their banks.

Sure, commercializing your blog is immoral, unethical, and uncool, but it's better than working as a waiter to fund your education. Just make sure you don't get Google pissed, or they'll drop you down in the search results and cripple your blog traffic. For the most part, blogging income is relatively secure, and easy to grow if you're web savvy and reasonably smart.

Check out *www.stevepavlina.com*, the online home of one of the world's leading personal development and blogging/website gurus. There you'll find lots of information to inspire you to "de-couple your value from your time" and start earning 24/7.

Cybersquatting

Buy up hundreds of celebrity domain names for cents and then display ads using these high profile names to generate revenue without having any association to them, but hurry. Tech-savvy NBA player Chris Bosh, star power forward for the Toronto Raptors, recently spoiled the party by winning a landmark legal case against Hoopology.com, and gained custody of his own domain name plus nearly 800 others and punitive damages.

SponsoredTweets

Earn money from your smartphone too. SponsoredTweets is a new Twitter advertising platform that connects advertisers with Tweeters. Advertisers can create sponsored conversations on Twitter. Tweeters can earn money for spreading the word. Don't have an account on SponsoredTweets? Create one now!

49. Get the Perfect Internship:

An internship is a great way for you to get your foot in the door of any company and gain work experience and important contacts without having to make a commitment. Finding the perfect internship requires research and determination, but getting it right can take you all the way to the top—getting jizzed on by the President himself.

Figure Out What You Want

There's no point applying for an internship until you have decided what you want from it, and how it will further your career goals. For example, if you want to be a movie actor, don't get an internship in a movie studio; aim for a restaurant management trainee program instead. Some internships, such as those in publicity and investment banking, are highly competitive, while other fields are more relaxed. Either way, all you'll be doing is fetching coffee and sorting the mail, so don't bust your balls at this stage. Always choose a paid internship, because unpaid is slavery, and class credits mean more work writing a paper about how you fetched coffee and sorted the mail.

Work Up Your Resume

You'll need to write a resume and a cover letter. Your resume should show that you have a passionate interest in counting paperclips and waiting in line at Starbucks. You need to demonstrate an ability to remember a twelve shot venti soy hazelnut vanilla cinnamon half-caf white mocha with extra white mocha plus eight other beverages, and make important decisions on your feet, like the best substitute for Carrot Passion Cake or Apple Fritter Donuts. All this experience may seem irrelevant now, but it will help you to be customer focused when you flunk your course and become a barista.

Fire Off Lots of Letters

Send out lots of letters and check internship websites like letsplayhidethecigar.com. If no positions are available, ask a company if they'll create one or let you stalk one of their employees during your summer break.

Stick It Out

You only get out of an internship what you are willing to put into it (and if you put out as well, even better). However, if your boss can't keep his fly shut, politely refuse all offers of complimentary dry cleaning vouchers. And remember, even if you hate what you're doing, it's all part of the realization that work sucks, so you may as well get used to it.

50. Fake Throwing Someone Out of a Window:

If you live in a hall where the rooms are very similar, this elaborate prank will convince a reasonably drunk victim they are being thrown to their death. The best time to do it is at night, and when the victim is already the center of attention, like a birthday, so he doesn't get suspicious of his "special" treatment.

Pick Your Victim

Your victim needs to live on the third floor or higher, otherwise the trick won't work. While one group of friends goes out to the bar with him, another group clears out his room, drags all his belongings down several flights of stairs, and then reassembles it in the identical room on the ground floor.

Get Your Victim Drunk

Mucho tequila shots later, it's time for everyone to stagger home. As you approach the halls, tell the birthday boy that you've got a surprise present, but he has to be blindfolded first. When you are sure he can't see, take him into the elevator and go up a few floors, then go down again (argue amongst yourselves about the joker who keeps pressing the wrong buttons); go up and down for a bit, until the victim is properly confused, then go to the ground floor.

Through the Door, Out the Window

Guide your charge into his fake bedroom, then take off his blindfold and crack open a bottle of champagne, or party poppers—anything to cause a distraction so he doesn't take too close a look around. Give him his surprise present (a tiny pair of wings wrapped inside a large box, a bungee rope, or anything that foreshadows throwing him out of the window). After he's expressed dismay at his slightly disturbing gift, announce that it's time for a test run. Open the window and hang him out feet first. Enjoy his pleading screams for a few minutes, then let go when his feet are a foot from the ground.

51. Screw Up Your Professor's Lecture:

Screwing up a lecture can be an individual mission or a group effort. The solo efforts won't help your grades, but they're still fun. The group attacks can subtly undermine the professor's concentration and self-confidence, so they don't even know they're being scammed, and can't make an example of any single person.

Text Your Friends

Get those fingers working; make sure every time he looks your way you've got your head down and fingers tapping away. When your professor asks a question, jump up and down waving your hands in the air and when she calls on you, say, "No, I wasn't raising my hand, I was trying to get a signal so I can send this text."

Rattle Your Jewelry

Wear armloads of bracelets that clank and jangle every time you move. Tell your professor you have to wear them as part of your religion. Make lots of noise.

Answer Questions

When you answer questions, begin with "And of course, that would to be . . ..". If you don't' know the answer say, "No, but your mom does." (This answer is applicable in a wide range of situations.)

Clear Your Throat Noisily

Then spit into your handkerchief. Explain that you are trying to follow the example of the holy anchorite saints by reserving swallowing for the Eucharist.

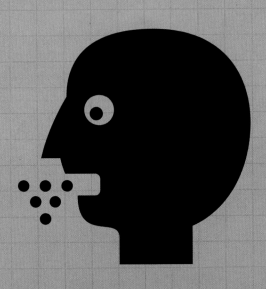

Act Dumb

Get everyone to adopt attentive, but dumb faces—slightly slack jawed, vacant look in the eyes. Don't overdo it though; you want the lecturer to believe that you really look like that. When he sees a crowd of dipshits staring back at him he will truly begin to question what he is doing with his life.

Group Frown

Everyone frowns slightly and stares at something non-existent above the professor's head.

Smelly Pits

Get the professor to question his or her personal hygiene by having all the students sitting in the front three rows make like there is a gag-inducing smell wafting toward them from the front of the room.

52. Survive the Roommate from Hell:

You may breeze through college and never meet the Roommate from Hell, but chances are you will wind up with one at least once during your four years. The best way to beat them is to recognize the tactics they use to get under your skin, and clearly assert your needs and feelings.

Stay Calm

Never lose your temper, even when your roommate is being an über-jerk. Losing your temper always puts you in the weaker position (especially if you resort to violence, which will land you in even bigger trouble). Stay calm and show that you are in control of your emotions, not him. When you get stressed or angry, you always hand others the power.

Whackos and Intimidators

Jerks usually fall into one of two categories: whackos or intimidators. Whackos are self-obsessed losers who feed on emotional attention and like to cause chaos around them by turning everything into a melodrama where they are the star. Intimidators try to gain power over others through fear, and make you doubt yourself. Even when regular messy roomies drive you nuts with their carelessness, they are still being manipulative, because they are affecting you emotionally, and you probably end up cleaning up their mess. Recognizing how you are being manipulated helps you to stay calm.

Stand Your Ground

Don't be a pushover. The worst thing you can do is compromise your needs just to avoid a conflict. If you feel they are making unreasonable demands, then take a stand and don't let them intimidate or talk you into feeling otherwise. Hellish roomies are master manipulators who are experts at shifting blame and responsibility off themselves and making others feel guilty.

Express Your Needs

Explain what behavior is acceptable and what is unacceptable. Draw up some house rules. If you don't take responsibility to set boundaries and set them out clearly, how can you expect others to stay within them? Always speak in person, rather than leaving notes on the fridge, which generally just increase friction or get ignored.

Get Them to Move Out

If you really can't live with your roommate, then make sure they move out. Why should you move when they're being so unreasonable? Tell them they've got a week to find a new place, and offer to help them move (so they can't guilt-trip you).

53. Pass Your Exams Without Studying:

Trying to pass an exam without studying is like trying to climb Everest without oxygen—it's technically possible but immensely difficult. If you screw up nobody will bother to airlift your frozen cadaver off the glacier, and if you succeed people will still think you're a dick. To be a successful student you have to demonstrate that you have a thorough understanding of the course's subject matter, but there are ways of doing this while actually knowing very little.

Expert Knowledge

If you're studying a science, you need to know the basics in order to build on your knowledge. However, since many of the humanities don't involve a pyramid-knowledge model, it is taken as a given that you will have read the set texts and know the basics, so you don't get any credit for showing this. So if you skip the basics you can still get a good grade by focusing on themes, and some very specific details that will impress your professor rather than put him to sleep like the boring stuff all the other students will regurgitate in their exams.

Focus on a handful of ideas and topics in great depth, so that you have a thorough understanding of them. When you demonstrate this expert knowledge, it implies that you have mastered the basic and intermediate stages that came before. It's like if you learned how to jump buses on your motorcycle, people would wrongly assume that you know how to properly shift gears.

Concentrate in Class

Go to every lecture, participate in seminars, and pay attention, take lots of detailed notes, and then read them again before you go to bed to understand and memorize the most important points. If you get the information into your brain on the same day you are presented with it, there's no need to cram it all in the day before the exam.

Practice Papers

Most fraternities and sororities have a collection of exam papers going back to the Declaration of Independence. If the same questions have come up six years in a row, there's a good chance they will appear on your exam. There are no guarantees, of course, but there's certainly no need to learn the whole syllabus if you can make some well-informed predictions.

54. Go Streaking Through the Quad:

In 1973 more than 500 students at the University of Maryland took part in a mass nude run. The event was unusual, but it was no secret; in fact, a local Washington DC news station covered the event. The naked runners streaked past the reporter but amazingly they didn't realize that's what they were doing, since the verb "streak" in its modern usage was about to be uttered for the first time (although they had been "running a streak" at Princeton since the mid-sixties). The reporter exclaimed, "They are streaking past me right now. It's an incredible sight!" and the lexicon was the better for it. Until then, and since as far back as the American Revolution, the word had meant "to go quickly, to rush, to run at full speed" with no mention of clothing.

The Origin of Campus Streaking

Despite lacking the words to express it, the phenomenon of dropping trough and running around the university campus can be traced back to 1804—they just had to wait another 169 years to give it a name. The first recorded college streak was made by George William Crump at Washington College (now Washington and Lee University), for which he was suspended for a semester. He later became a U.S. Congressman and Ambassador.

There are lots of formalized streaking traditions at American colleges. At Harvard, they call it Primal Scream, when students streak through the Old Yard at midnight right before finals start; Lewis & Clark College is proud to host the naked mile parade on prospective student weekend. There is also a Naked Quad Run every year at Tufts. So if you decide to get naked and run around a bit, you're in good company.

Safety in Numbers

The more of you take part, the less chance you'll get caught or make a scene. One person showing his junk is an indecent act—twenty people doing it is a flash mob. Make sure you hide a spare set of clothes somewhere along your route, in case your route back to your starting point becomes impassable.

Check the Law in Your Area

Public indecency laws are being more zealously enforced these days. Streakers can be arrested and placed on the sex offenders registry for life under Megan's Law. Check the legal implications of being arrested for showing your tackle in your college's jurisdiction, as it may be different from what you are used to back home. If you're worried about getting arrested, tie your underwear around your head like a bandana, so if the cops arrive you can dive into a bush and make yourself somewhat decent.

55. Get Away with Not Doing Homework:

Sitting at a desk staring at a blank screen and worrying about all the homework you're not doing sucks. Sitting at a desk actually doing your homework sucks even more, so stop being conscientious and start making excuses to your professors and to yourself.

Make the Lie Big

Nobody would insult their professor's intelligence by saying their dog ate their homework unless it were really true. The bigger the lie, the more plausible it becomes. As Adolf Hitler knew well, "Make the lie big, make it simple, keep saying it, and eventually they will believe it."

Dutch forger and unappreciated artist Han van Meegeren conned the art world with his Vermeer forgeries by exploiting something called "confirmation bias." This is an irrational tendency to search for, interpret, or remember information in a way that confirms preconceptions or a working hypothesis. Since the "my dog ate it" is such a clichéd excuse, confirmation bias actually works in reverse, so no one will doubt you.

Keep It Simple

Everyone knows that good liars base their lies on the truth, bad liars embellish and provide too many details, and truth tellers keep things simple. So excuses like "I left it at home, and have forgotten where I live" or "The dog ate my printer" are more effective than elaborate yarns. However, be prepared to provide details if required.

Body Language

Don't cover your face or scratch your nose while you are lying to your professor, as this will telegraph that you are making it up. Instead, scratch your butt, rattle your keys, and keep good eye contact. Look up and to the left (which makes you look like you're accessing memories rather than lying). Be cooperative but don't smile—it is almost impossible to fake a smile, so don't bother, it will only give you away. Keep your eyes relaxed because the scared bug-eyed look is a dead giveaway.

Believe Your Lie

As George Costanza once advised Jerry Seinfeld, "Jerry, just remember, it's not a lie if you believe it." The best liars convince even themselves that they are telling the truth.

Stay Calm

Liars always give themselves away by feeling stressed, or trying to fake a feeling of calmness, which makes them freeze up and look stiff and unspontaneous. Stay calm and stop caring about what your professor thinks of you. The less you care about people's opinions, the easier it is to lie to them.

56. Get Someone Else to Do Your Laundry:

There are three kinds of people who can do your laundry: parents, lovers, and roommates. Love and fear are the best motivators, so use them to your advantage and you can catch up on some studying, get a better grade, better job, and then one day you can pay someone to do your dirty work forever.

Take It Home

Store it up, take it home, get your mom to do it—and not to be sexist, your dad should do his fair share too. Maybe he can scrub the stains off your duvet covers. This takes some planning, the least of which is that you've got to have enough clothes to last you between trips home. You can make a pair of underwear last a week—the correct way; inside out the correct way; right-side out backwards; inside-out backwards. When your folks baulk at the sight of you struggling across the threshold with a laundry basket that looks like Jabba the Hutt, remind them how much college is costing them and ask which they would prefer to do: pay for you to study or to do laundry?

Love Washes Everything

Love is a beautiful feeling, which becomes all the more appealing when your partner would rather do all your laundry than risk you suffering an obsessive compulsive relapse. Have the "we need to talk" talk. Confess that you suffer from OCD, and ask a big favor. You've got handwashing down to thirty times a day, but you are scared that if you start doing your own laundry you'll suffer a relapse. Life is just starting to look good again, the future is bright, you don't want to go back there. "So will you do this one little thing for me—twice a week? I don't know what I'd do without you—take these quarters, I insist."

Con Your Roommate

You have just heard there's an escaped prison on the loose around the campus and the safest place for your roommate is in the basement. "Oh and take my laundry with you seeing as you're going anyway. I'll barricade myself in here and keep your Xbox safe. Go, quickly! Save yourself before it's too late."

57. Write a Term Paper in Five Minutes:

This powerful technique enables anyone to write a term paper in 300 seconds by focusing on the matter at hand using the universal principle that even a four-year-old can concentrate really hard for five minutes.

Minute One

Write a sentence of introduction stating what your term paper is about. Grab the reader with its breathtaking succinctness. Some people prefer to leave writing the introduction to the end, when they have a clearer idea of the contents of the paper. If you have any time left at the end of the first minute, check your emails.

Minute Two

Write a three-sentence thesis statement. This is the subject of the term paper and should clearly expand upon the sentence you have written in the introduction. If you have decided to leave the introduction until last, skip this for now and move on to Step 3.

Minute Three

Use four sentences to express four ideas that are key to your paper. Don't worry about grammar or spelling at this stage. Just get your ideas down. If inspiration doesn't strike, or you are experiencing eye strain, don't waste time staring at a blank screen; just move on to the next step and return to this later.

Minute Four

Write a three-sentence conclusion presenting the results generated by the key ideas (but only only if you have completed Steps 1 to 3).

Minute Five

Cut and paste a listmania bibliography from Amazon.com. If you haven't already, write the Introduction and correct your spelling. Reread your work and delete all, redundant or superfluous verbage. Finally, and most important of all, insert a header into your document stating: I KNOW THAT YOU ARE HAVING AN AFFAIR WITH [Insert Fellow Student's Name Here]. UNLESS YOU GIVE ME AN A, I WILL REPORT YOU TO THE DEAN.

58. Plagiarize Without Getting Caught:

The word plagiarism comes from the Latin *plagium,* which means "kidnapping"—a Federal offense, so no wonder it is such a big issue. When your professors were in college they had to walk to the library, read heaps of books, and then write their papers on stone tablets with a chisel. So imagine how jealous they must be of your generation who can download entire papers from the Internet without leaving their dorm and pass off paragraphs of copy-and-pasted text as their own.

Act Like an "A" Student

It is a common misconception that only mediocre or lazy students plagiarize, so no one will suspect you if you maintain the facade of a hard working, reliable student, who attends class regularly and takes part in discussions.

Start from the Beginning

Plagiarize from the very first week of your college career. Don't wait until you are juggling deadlines at the end of the semester, unless you want your writing style and that of your source material to invite comparison. If your early assignments contain sentences like "I think Freud's theory of gender is a bit dumb and that he needed to get out more" your professor will be rightly suspicious if a subsequent paper asserts: "Klein believes that a rudimentary ego is present from the beginning, capable of certain defensive strategies designed to protect a pre-symbolic, prelinguistic self."

Dumb It Down

Replace any big words that you don't understand or aren't part of your natural vocabulary with simpler ones. This is time consuming, and you will have to use an online dictionary, but it is well worth the extra effort. You don't want to be asked to define "phenomenological" the next time your graded paper is handed back to you. Also pepper the text with clumsy grammatical errors such as dangling participles ("After rotting in the cellar for weeks, my brother brought up some oranges") or tautology (repetition, such as "adequate enough").

Play Away from Home

Don't steal from your professor's own doctoral dissertation, or others prominent in the field. Most professors have an encyclopaedic knowledge of their peers' work so always mooch from lesser-known academics who nobody gives a crap about.

Launder the Text

When your assignment is complete, launder the text by copying it into Notepad to eliminate inconsistent formatting, hidden hyperlinks, font markers, and other unwanted metadata. Copy the text back into a Word document and manually replace formatting such as italics and bold.

Check Your Work

Your faculty probably uses plagiarism-checking software as routine, so steal similar software from a Torrent site and run your tweaked text through it to flag anything you might have overlooked.

Document Search Complete

59. Become the Big Man on Campus:

It's a commonly known fact that women are more attracted to the Big Man on Campus (BMOC) than any other male. He is the dominant Alpha Male in his peer group; he has a buffed physique, but he doesn't spend all his time in the gym; he is tall and handsome, but he can pass a mirror without checking himself out; he wears stylish clothes and isn't afraid to get his wallet out, but he isn't flashy. Not many people can naturally fill the role, which means that if you follow these four simple rules and act like an Alpha, you can increase your status, and maybe even reach the top of the pile.

Assume High Status

When you walk in the room do you look around for someone to follow, or do you take the lead and demand respect from everyone you meet? The BMOC knows that he is a natural leader and takes charge of every situation. Don't try to please people, or lower your status to make them feel more comfortable. As Marianne Williamson said, "Your playing small does not serve the world. There is nothing enlightened about shrinking so that other people won't feel insecure around you."

Be Cocky and Funny

Cocky sexual humor is a big turn on (so long as it isn't crass or offensive) because it projects the image of a cool, relaxed man-in-charge. But you've got to have both together: Being cocky without the humor is arrogance; being funny without the cockiness just makes you the dorky comedy guy. Teasing women, busting their balls, being funny and a bit arrogant shows them that you are the boss. They may say they hate you for being a chauvinistic male, but they'll be secretly attracted.

Be Confident

Confidence is hard to fake, but not impossible. Just remember that all interactions between men are informed by the question "Which one of us would win a fight?" You won't be aware that you are doing it, but it is hardwired into your subconscious, because thousands of years ago it was directly relevant to survival. Now we're not suggesting you go throwing your weight around, especially in situations which are charged with testosterone and competition for females, such as bars and clubs, but don't defer to other males just because you have a glass jaw or don't know how to throw or take a punch. The majority of social interactions do not descend into violence, so don't make playing the tough guy your default setting.

Take the Lead

Make decisions. Know what you want. If you don't get what you want, don't complain or seek sympathy. Learn from your mistakes and take responsibility for yourself. Don't seek consensus—lead the group. For example, if you're at a bar and it's time to move on, don't ask, "What do you guys think? Shall we go somewhere else?" Take charge and say, "Right. Drink up guys, it's time to move on. Let's go to [Insert Bar Name Here]."

60. Avoid Getting Crabs:

Although you are unlikely to catch crabs from a toilet seat, there are many easier ways to become infected. If you or your roomie are sexually active you are at risk.

Pubic Lice

Crabs, also known as pubic lice, are tiny parasitic insects that camp out in your pubic hair. You can catch them through sexual contact, but also through infected clothing, towels, and bedding. You can tell if you have them because about five days after being infected your groin will start itching, especially at night when the lice stick their heads into your pubic hair follicles to feed on your blood.

Crabs are large enough to be seen with the naked eye, but they are easily mistaken for flakes of skin. Under a microscope they appear as tiny translucent crablike insects. Go to the doctor to confirm if you have crabs. Don't ignore the symptoms because left untreated crabs can develop into a serious skin infection, plus you'll spread it around. Crabs can also infest the eyebrows or eyelashes, causing the eyes to become inflamed.

Crab Avoidance

The best way to avoid crabs is to limit your number of sexual partners. A latex condom will reduce the risk of pregnancy and other STDs, but someone with crabs in their pubes can easily transfer them to yours regardless of whether you are rubbered up. Contrary to popular myth, you are very unlikely to catch crabs from a toilet seat. They can't live for long away from the warmth of the human body, and those that fall from the body are usually injured or dying.

Crab Treatment

If you or your roommate has crabs, you need to get rid of all lice and lice eggs (nits). Fortunately, you won't need to shave your pubic hair, but you will need to treat the area with an over-the-counter medicated cream and lice shampoo for milder cases, or something stronger for bigger infestations. Wetting the hairs with vinegar and combing with a nit comb will remove most of the eggs. Clothes, bedding, towels, upholstery, and other infected items must be machine washed on a hot setting, or if they can't be washed, left in a sealed plastic bag for 72 hours. Vacuum the mattress, pillow, couch, and floor, and don't have sex until you have completed the course of treatment.

Tell Everyone

Yeah buddy—sing it from the rooftops that you're subletting your khakis. You must inform everyone you've had sexual contact with recently, so they can get checked out as well.

61. Pretend You're Pre-Med:

There might be some advantages to pretending to be pre-med. It's possible you might attract a few gold-digging students by your massive earnings potential, but most students are more into having a good time now. This is really just a sociological experiment to improve your work ethic and help you empathize with pre-meds, who, after all, will one day be responsible for turning you away from the ER because you have no healthcare.

Give Up All Your Hobbies

Don't have any extra-curricular interests. The only way to get straight As is to spend countless hours as a study drone. That shouldn't stop you from joining lots of societies and trying to hold as many positions of responsibility as possible. Even though you'll blow everyone off when you're too busy studying, it will look great on your resume. Take Adderall, Provigil, Dexedrine, and Ritalin with every meal.

Only Learn What's on the Exam

You didn't go to college to learn and explore—you are here to ace exams; everything else is irrelevant. If anyone tries to engage you in a discussion about anything that isn't on the exam, don't waste your breath. Any spirit of curiosity in you is a dead giveaway that you're not thinking like a pre-med. Always favor memorizing stuff over understanding the underlying principles.

Be Arrogant and Complain about the Syllabus

Argue every point with your professor to bump up your grade, even if you don't deserve it. Drop the class if it looks like you're not going to get an A. Cheat on exams, and complain that your courses require you to learn pointless details you just won't need when you're a doctor, like identifying a pneumothorax on a chest radiograph, recognizing when a patient needs to be transferred to the ICU, or knowing how to perform CPR. If you wanted to learn that stuff you'd have become a nurse. Assume that anyone who isn't pre-med is wasting their time and will be unemployable, and that those going for liberal arts degrees will soon be eating up your tax dollars on welfare.

62. Graduate Early:

If you're sick of hemorrhaging money, or maybe you just want to be out in the real world being financially independent, or spend your fourth year traveling, then you should consider doing whatever it takes to graduate early. Planning a fast-track college career can even begin in high school, and requires focused commitment from Day One.

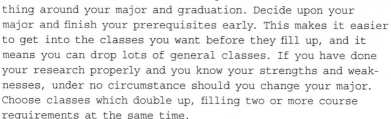

Know What You Want

Nail down your courses quickly, don't take any course that doesn't count for credits, and center everything around your major and graduation. Decide upon your major and finish your prerequisites early. This makes it easier to get into the classes you want before they fill up, and it means you can drop lots of general classes. If you have done your research properly and you know your strengths and weaknesses, under no circumstance should you change your major. Choose classes which double up, filling two or more course requirements at the same time.

Work Consistently

At the end of a college year, if you added up the time many students actually spent working, it would be surprisingly low.

Have you noticed how much time your friends spend thinking, talking, and complaining about assignments instead of actually doing them? By working consistently, every day, including vacations, you can fit three years' work into one. Forget internships—you can earn far more credits by taking more courses.

Be Healthy

Stay away from alcohol and drugs, eat healthily, and exercise regularly. Just one bender a week can reduce your productivity by a half. If you get smashed on a Friday night, your brain won't be borderline functional again until the middle of the following week. If you resist the temptations of booze and drugs (even coffee), you will be so clear headed your professors will think you are Galileo compared to your beer-swilling, pot-smoking peers.

Community College Transferable Credits

These courses are a little easier, but credits are credits. Get your college to agree during writing that your community college course credits are transferable, and then take some classes online in the summer. You can even do some of these courses while you are still in high school, and take some AP and IB exams. Many colleges accept AP credit if you score 3 or higher, and IB is accepted at many international colleges.

63. Make College Last Forever:

If someone asking you, "So, what are you going to do after you graduate?" causes physical pain, you don't need a doctor to tell you have a Van Wilder complex. If you take enough drugs you can make time stop for a while, but there are other ways of staying in college forever, even after your parents decide to cut you adrift. Simply get industry fat cats to give you a truckload of backhanders to do biased research in key areas.

Kill Google

If your PhD thesis is called "Ways to make Google bend over and take it up the ass," Steve Ballmer will personally hand deliver a suitcase full of cash to your dorm every week. You'll have so much mullah stuffed under your mattress you'll be sleeping on the ceiling.

Peak Oil

Oil companies pay big bucks to academics to prop up the myth that the world is running out of the black stuff, so OPEC can restrict supply and hike up the price. Also required is research into even more far-fetched ways of getting it out of the ground, so when prices at the pumps stay high despite a slump in the global oil price, oil companies can say they are pumping all their profits into research and development (that's you buddy).

Global Warming

The big one—it's here, and we all knew it was coming, along with huge chunks of Antarctic ice and—get this—great gobs of cash heading into the pockets of anyone who can tell us whether we're going to flood, freeze, or fry, and how quickly it will happen. There are now so many hurricanes that you can get a grant just to count them. For thirty years the scientists have been telling us we're screwed, but it's only now that you can get mucho dinero to stay in college to study the global impact of reusing party toothpicks and mulching your lawn clippings.

Drug Companies

In 2002, the combined profits for the top ten drug companies in the Fortune 500 were more than for all the other 490 businesses put together. Wouldn't you like a slice of that rancid pie? Clinical studies sponsored by pharmaceutical companies are so routinely biased that weak data and marketing dressed up as research can keep you in Bud Lite and beer nuts for the rest of your days.

64. Kidnap the Dean:

Congratulations for contemplating the *Mission: Impossible* of college pranks—kidnapping the Dean. It is probably unlike anything you have done before. If you have never kidnapped a member of the faculty then you may have doubts about your expertise in this area. You'll also worry whether you'll end up wearing an orange jumpsuit for the next decade.

What's the Time?

Before committing any federal felony, it's worth familiarizing yourself with the penalties. Society doesn't look kindly on the forcible and unlawful detention of another against their will. However, so long as you stick to "vanilla" kidnapping, and don't get tempted into blackmail, extortion, sexual assault or threats to kill, you're probably looking at eight to ten if you use a firearm, keep the Dean for an extended period, or demand ransom money. It's probably safest to stick to a blindfold and duct tape, let him or her go free after a week, and demand something other than money (like free Ben & Jerry's for everyone on campus— which will get them on your side when Kevin Spacey arrives to conduct negotiations).

It's So Easy

Few students realize how easy it is to kidnap the Dean. If they did, no doubt he or she would get abducted every day, and would find it very difficult to fulfil his or her faculty responsibilities, which must be considerable. As with most crimes, the most important factor is the element of surprise, but since most people don't expect to get kidnapped, any time will do.

Other Supplies

Plan ahead and purchase some extra supplies to accommodate your new charge. Your budget can't be expected to extend to traditional faculty fare like white truffles and lobster thermidor, but you can't reasonably expect a man or woman of letters to survive on your diet of Pop Tarts and Gatorade. Being duct taped underneath your bed for a week will be culture shock enough, regardless of dietary preferences.

Stockholm Syndrome

It is common for abducted hostages to develop a strong emotional attachment to their hostage-taker. This can be used to your advantage, to bump up your grades or get special permission to use a toaster in your dorm, but don't exploit the situation and enter into a physical relationship. Keep the abduction strictly professional so there is less chance of you leading the Dean on, or lying about your feelings so as not to offend.

65. Elevator Surf:

Elevator surfing does not require a wetsuit, you can't get attacked by sharks, you won't get knocked unconscious by a big wave, yet the practice of riding on top of an elevator, or jumping from one to another seems to have acquired a notoriety quite out of proportion to its danger. It's probably illegal, which means you need to stay alive and avoid detection.

Halt the Elevator Between Floors

Head to the elevators very early in the morning while the place is deserted. Board the elevator and press the "Stop" button while it is between floors. This may set off an alarm. If so, press "Start" and postpone your attempt to another day. Next time you will need to stop the elevator between floors by

prising open the internal doors to trip the safety stop mechanism. Once the elevator is held between two floors, open the internal doors and then undo the latch mechanism to open the external doors. Crawl out and then climb on top of the elevator. Alternatively you can open the exterior doors on the floor above and jump down or slide down the cable from there. If you can't get your hands on an elevator key, you'll have to simply force the external doors open from the outside.

Operate the Elevator

You should be able to control the elevator by using the control box on top of the elevator. The box will have several buttons and switches. Flick the one labeled "Inspection" or "Maintenance." This will disable the controls in the rest of the building, so that the elevator will only move under your manual control. Look for a "Run/Stop" switch, and flick it into the "Stop" position. Climb on top of the elevator and operate using the "Up/Down" switch. You may have to simultaneously press a safety switch to override the system. After you've had your fun, remember to put the elevator back into "Normal" mode.

Explore

Elevator surfing allows you to explore areas and even entire floors that might otherwise be off limits. At the top or bottom of the shaft, look for an entrance to the elevator mechanical room. That may lead you onto the roof or into a sub-basement. Or simply place the elevator into "Normal" mode and eavesdrop on people's conversations. Oh, and make sure you don't get your head cut off by the counterweight.

66. Get College Credits by Playing Video Games and Watching *Star Trek* and Porn:

There's always talk about how college education has been dumbed down year after year, so it's reassuring to remind ourselves that there are still colleges offering quality courses in *Star Trek*, *StarCraft* and X-rated entertainment. Here are some classes that demonstrate how a liberal-arts education remains an excellent investment.

Star Trek

Georgetown University in Washington D.C. offers a course called "Philosophy and Star Trek" as a way to explore some of the fundamental ideas of philosophy. Over at Indiana University Bloomington you can take "*Star Trek* and Religion" as an "introduction to the critical study of religion by way of popular culture."

Learning from YouTube

Pitzer College in Southern California hosts a for-credit
media studies class where students watch YouTube videos, discuss them, and leave comments on the site. Way to dovetail
work and play. As you might expect, the classes themselves are
recorded and then posted on YouTube.

Mail Order Brides

Johns Hopkins University offers "Mail Order Brides: Understanding the Philippines in Southeast Asian Context." It
examines Filipino kinship and gender stereotyping, though
students are discouraged from sampling the merchandise.

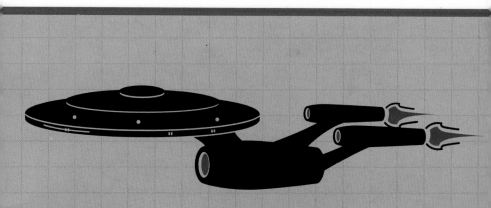

Porn

Several colleges offer courses about pornography (and you thought it was a self-taught skill). The State University of New York at Buffalo offers "Cyberporn and Society," University of California Berkeley offers "Cinema and the Sex Act," and if discussing X-rated Japanese comic books floats your junk, head to New York University for "Anthropology of the Unconscious." All these courses get students thinking about porn, rather than mindlessly beating off to it, which has to be a good thing.

Walking

Kentucky's Center College's new class, the "Art of Walking," explores how Immanuel Kant's Critique of Judgment reveals "a pleasure apparently foreign to aesthetics but very much at home in human nature: the pleasure of walking" around the Danville, Kentucky area, including strolls through "nature preserves, battlefields, cemeteries, the nearby Shaker Village, campuses and farms."

StarCraft

The University of California Berkeley uses "The Strategy of StarCraft" to teach the art of war, strategy and tactics, and presumably have a laugh at all those losers in South Korea who make it their career or watch it on TV.

67. Survive Spring Break:

A young Benjamin Franklin once declared, "Temperance, chastity, and moderation—screw those, I'm hitching to Key West to get wasted and see me some hooters." He was, of course, referring to Spring Break when thousands of students seeking nightlife, liberty, and the pursuit of happy hour head to party hotspots like Florida, Mexico, or South Padre Island to join a sizzling scene where sandy beaches play host to margarita mayhem. So it's no surprise that the Canadians have invented their own name for this wild oasis of pleasure: Reading Week. If you want to catch up with some

coursework and survive Spring Break without getting thrown in jail, catching an STD, or binging on booze or drugs, just ask yourself: "What would Benjamin Franklin do?"

Fort Liquorfree, Florida

Once Spring Break party central, the Venice of America, Fort Lauderdale had a makeover in the early '90s so now it's more beach chic than drunken chicks. Jog briskly along the palm tree-fringed beachfront promenade, or check out Stranahan house, the oldest building in the city, originally built as a trade post. Sadly it's too hot for ice hockey here, but at the International Swimming Hall of Fame and Aquatic Complex you might be able to catch a future Olympic champion swim some laps, take a few sips of isotonic fluid, nibble a banana, and then swim a bit more.

Daytona Beach, Florida

Daytona is the home of NASCAR, officially the most boring sport in the world. Its wide expanse of smooth, compacted sand makes it one of the few ocean beaches that a car can be driven on, but best avoided if you want to squeeze another 6,000 miles from your brake linings. So start your engines and cruise carefully to the Daytona 500 Experience where you can enjoy its ample parking and then marvel at thought-provoking race-used memorabilia.

South Padre Island, Texas

South Padre Island is named for a Catholic priest, Padre José Nicolás Ballí. Take communion, or rent a boat and go fishing or dolphin watching; sign up for an ecological tour to explore Padre Island National Seashore.

Panama City Beach, Florida

This place actually welcomes spring breakers, so stay right away from its 27 miles of beach parties and bikini-clad lady bumps. Don't be seduced by the wet T-shirt competitions, drinking contests, rock and rap stars, and 24/7 party insanity. It's hardly the Christian and Missionary Alliance, and those summer exams are fast approaching, aren't they?

68. Gain the Respect of Your Professors:

Making a good impression on your professors not only improves your grades, it sets you up after you graduate because you'll need someone to write a reference when you apply for your first job. If your professors don't even remember your name, then you need to work on your attitude, which requires a simple mind shift. It's not about you, it's about them. Once you realize that professors share our human frailties, pandering to their egos and propping up their flagging sense of self-worth is a much more active and achievable goal than simply trying not to flunk their classes.

How to Validate Someone's Existence

Professors need to be loved, feel respected and valued, and to believe that joining the disappointing ranks of academia was a worthwhile life choice. They have made many sacrifices to reach the top, only to find that the world now honors celebrities rather than philosophers. The best way to boost their self-esteem is to start an affair (see page 39), or simply lead them on:

Show Up to Class

Professors notice which students turn up regularly to class, but you can help by sitting in the same place and dressing like them. They'll be flattered that not only do you find them mentally stimulating, but you also look to them for fashion inspiration.

Take Part

Many professors factor your participation into your final grade, so make sure you take part in class discussions, even if it's only to disagree with everyone else with your poorly-researched and intellectually flimsy opinions.

Listen

Paying attention to what someone else is saying is the best way to let them think they matter. Make frequent eye contact, and use gestures like nodding your head, smiling, or grabbing yourself to show that you are literally being touched by their intellect.

Present Yourself Professionally

Put on some proper clothes, rather than your pajama pants, and keep new fangled technology like your iPod or iPhone out of sight, as this reminds your professor about their youth misspent cramming for exams. You have your whole life ahead of you—don't rub it in with a piece of hardware they can't understand or afford.

Positive Feedback

Tell your professor which parts of the course you found most interesting or challenging. This helps them to feel less of a mid-life malfunction. The thrill of tenure and a position for life will have worn off decades ago, so any positive signs that they deserve to keep their job are very welcome.

69. Survive a Semester Abroad:

What we really mean here is survive a semester in Europe. Travel broadens the mind, so when you really get to know a foreign culture the first thing you'll realize about national stereotyping is that it's spot on. After all, if it wasn't true it wouldn't exist. But in case you don't want to spend your time thinking about national stereotypes—we've done it to save you the bother. To save space we haven't included Italy, but would like to point out that it has the most corrupt politicians in Europe but the best weather.

United Kingdom

All you have to know to get on in the UK is that their beer is warm, but they don't care because they spend most of the time tipping it over their heads and drinking each other's urine. England is full of fifty-somethings growing honeysuckle and moaning constantly about noise and cars and schedule changes on Radio 4, while their behaviorally challenged teenagers perform handbrake turns in the parking lot of McDonald's in their customized Vauxhall Novas. In their favor, their love of eating offal (entrails and internal organs) is second only to the Scottish. Don't bother visiting Wales, where they think they are a nation of poets and singers when in reality they are a bunch of unemployed minors and alcoholics. You aren't missing much culturally if you skip over it during your travels. The Americans have the Smithsonian; the French have the Louvre; the Spanish have the Prado; the Italians have the Uffizi; the Welsh have the National Slate Museum at Llanberis.

France

The French seem to love speaking French and are reluctant to speak English. Their language is full of impenetrable grammar and hyperbolic pouting. For example, "what a shame" translates to "quel catastrophe!" in French. They don't even have their own words for most things (not surprising for a nation that has elevated gesticulating to an art form). For example, the French for chewing gum is "le chewing gum." French women braid their underarm hair, they all think Jerry Lewis is a comic genius, and they invented sadism, the guillotine, student riots, and the metric system. Even though their national drink, *pastis*, tastes like mouthwash, nobody over the age of fifty has more than six teeth left. And nobody in France is allowed to work more than 35 hours a week. This explains why they are so reluctant to get involved in any acts of war (except for nuking Pacific islands and blowing up Greenpeace ships), since war involves heaps of overtime and interferes with lunch. Most of the country is on strike anyway.

Germany

You can drive at any speed without fear of getting caught, but get arrested for jaywalking at 2 A.M. across a deserted street. And that's not the only crappy thing about the country. German toilets pander to the national obsession for turd watching. You have to dump on a dry ledge and then flush repeatedly to remove even the smallest log. Though they did invent the hamburger but also started WWII (and harbor a collective guilt over it). These advancements led to the US becoming the fattest yet most prosperous nation in the world.

Spain

If you plan on studying abroad in Spain, you better enjoy the late-nightlife. You won't be heading to the discothèque until 1 A.M. after filling up on fish, wine, and secondhand smoke. Then you'll be packed into a club with loud music and louder people, who don't know the definition of personal space. Don't worry about being tired the next day. You only have to make it until mid-afternoon before everything shuts down for siesta, and everyone goes home to go to sleep.

70. Sabotage a College Football Game:

There are lots of dirty tricks that you can use to distract players and the fans of the opposing team, and only one of them involves taking off your clothes.

Laser Quest

Laser-pointers can be purchased online for very cheap and are very easy to conceal, although you have to be quite close to the play to be effective. Shine your laser into the quarterback's eyes and watch him get sacked by your linebackers. Your closest target will often be the wide receiver, so blast him with some rays just as he is setting up to catch a pass.

Streaking

Running around the field naked will disrupt the game for as long as it takes the biggest lineman you have ever seen to shoulder check you so hard you detach both retinas and wake

up to find you've had seven hours of facial reconstruction
surgery. If you're a woman, you probably won't get treated
so roughly, but those jocks still won't take kindly to having
their game interrupted.

Rose Bowl Hoax

Neil Steinberg, author of *If At All Possible Involve a Cow:
The Book of College Pranks*, writes that "few college pranks
can be said to be more grandly conceived, carefully planned,
flawlessly executed, and publicly dramatic" than the 1961 Rose
Bowl Hoax. Pull off your own version by tampering with the
flip-card routine. Pose as a reporter and interview the head
cheerleader, who will be only too happy to reveal the intri-
cate details of the flip-card system. Break into the cheerleaders' rooms and steal the master instruction sheet, and then
print off a couple thousand exact duplicates. Mark them up by
hand, then sneak back into the cheerleaders' rooms and do a
switcheroo.

Kidnap the Mascot

Sucker punch the opposing team's mascot, and then pass
the semi-conscious body around for some impromptu crowd
surfing. Before returning him to the field, superglue the
fastenings so he has to be cut out of the costume after
suffering a heat stroke.

Grease the Tracks

Resurrect Auburn University's nineteenth-century tradition of greasing the local railway tracks, causing the train

bringing the opposing team into town to overshoot the station by several miles, giving them an energy-sapping trek back to your campus. (Or you could try and mess with their bus' route, since most teams don't travel by train anymore.)

Inflatable Fun

On October 18, 2009, a boy threw a beach ball onto the field during an English soccer game between Sunderland and Liverpool. A Sunderland striker kicked the soccer ball and it deflected off the beach ball to score a goal. The referee let the goal stand, Liverpool lost the game 1-0, and the beach ball was hailed as the "beach ball of God." Alternatively you could copy the MIT prank at the 1982 Harvard/Yale game by causing a weather balloon to pop out from under the field and burst in an explosion of talcum powder. You'll need a prion-driven hydraulic press and a vacuum cleaner motor wired into an empty circuit breaker on the irrigation control board to inflate the balloon, as well as eight secret nighttime trips to the stadium and about twenty of the country's top technical brains. Better to stick with the beach ball.

71. Sell Your Organs for Beer Money:

Selling your organs can be a great way to make some extra money because one person's viscera is another person's vitality. Right now, about 90,000 men, women, and children in America need organ transplants and about sixteen people die every day because they don't get one, so it's practically your duty to offload some of your innards to subsidize your next kegger.

Is It Ethical?

Does the Pope shit in the woods? Of course it's ethical. What could be more ethical than a person of sound mind and body living in a liberal democracy and free market economy deciding they want beer more than one of their kidneys? A sick person wants a kidney more than money, so it's a mutually beneficial exchange, and after your fifth bottle of beer these ethical dilemmas become less important anyhow.

Is It Legal?

Are polar bears Catholic? No—the law forbids any money or other "valuable considerations" from changing hands in exchange for an organ donation. Also, more importantly, most organs may be donated only if a person is declared brain dead. That's precisely the reason why an illegal black market dealing organs is thriving, especially on college campuses, since dying rich people will pay huge sums to get their hands on tender young organs. Flip through the pages of any fashion magazine to see that the commodization of human bodies is already thriving, so what's the big deal?

Is It Painful?

Did flash-forwards ruin Season Four of *Lost*? Of course it's painful. Having a kidney removed is not only difficult and dangerous, it hurts a lot. Also, if your remaining kidney fails you, you're dead. And a month after the operation, you'll be in so much pain you'll wish the surgeon had removed both kidneys.

Have Kidney Will Travel

To have your organs harvested, you will likely have to go abroad where the rules are less strict. The number one destination is probably China because its government openly condones organ harvesting. Hospitals there headhunt foreigners and are prepared to pay up to $65,000 for a kidney. Also, check out Moldova, where the government has issued a ban but it is also directly involved with the trade. Other topnotch organ-trafficking destinations include India, Pakistan, Egypt, Israel, Russia, Singapore, Philippines, Colombia, Turkey, South Korea, and Taiwan.

72. Compete in a Prank War with a Rival College:

Practical jokes pulled by rival colleges—it's a recipe for things to spiral horribly out of control because the key is escalation as each prank gets crueller than the one before. Once the tipping point has been reached, it can only be stopped when someone gets arrested or killed. So think long and hard before you spawn a monster. There will be blood and this is how it plays out.

Phase 1

It starts off so innocently. You call up a pizza delivery place and order twenty pizzas for the captain of the football team at your rival college. They have to pay for a bunch of food they don't want and a couple of cheerleaders who were hanging out with him get tipped over the edge and check into rehab to address their bulimia. Lesson: The results always exceed the intended goal.

Phase 2

So the jock captain guy gets a bunch of his bovine teammates and they sneak over to your college in the middle of the night to take a dump on the statue of your illustrious founder. Their nasty pieces of crap are so full of Nandrolone and assorted horse steroids that the next morning those babies are practically walking around the campus by themselves. Lesson: Fecal matter always comes into play quicker than you'd expect.

Phase 3

It just got personal, not to mention unhygienic, so your next move is to call the authorities and tell them that the captain's brother, who is sleeping on his couch, is an illegal immigrant. They storm his frat house with a SWAT team, and what do you know—the guy's brother is an illegal after all. Not your fault. How were you to know? By now the guy is really pissed. Lesson: You mess with his family, it gets ramped up another notch.

Phase 4

So the jock captain guy calls his uncle who works at a top secret research laboratory. He sneaks over to your college in the middle of the night wearing a full biohazard suit and releases anthrax into the air conditioning system of twenty of the biggest buildings on campus, which kills eighty percent of the students. Lesson: This is where it gets deadly.

Phase 5

You retaliate by detonating the hydrogen bomb you've been building in your physics class. Lesson: College prank wars can lead to World War III; don't say you weren't warned.

73. Binge Drink on a Budget:

Binge drinking—drinking alcohol solely for the purpose of intoxication—can be quite a challenge when you're on a tight budget. Shots, chugging, and drinking games don't come cheap. If you are worried that poor cash flow is interfering with your drinking, look out for these signs: attending class, engaging in planned or safe sexual activity, waking up without any inexplicable injuries or Sharpie ink on your face. If this sounds familiar, it may be time to rediscover some old fashioned methods of getting totally pixilated.

Drink Through a Straw

Drinking alcohol through a straw actually makes no difference to how quickly you get drunk, but your body doesn't know this. Conditioned in its formative years by the placebo effect, the residual memory of how drinking through a straw used to make you feel when you were underage should be sufficient to get you wasted quickly.

Quit Smoking

Research has shown that smoking diminishes the effects of alcohol by reducing the amount that reaches the intestine where it is absorbed into the bloodstream. So if you want to get properly blacked out, go easy on the butts. It leaves you more money for booze, and your gut can get on with the business of getting you hooched up.

Empty Stomach

Don't bother eating before you go out. Drinking on an empty stomach is the best way to make you drunk. Dr. Guy Ratcliffe, medical director of the Medical Council on Alcoholism, explains: "Alcohol is a very simple molecule and is absorbed very rapidly. If you have a full stomach, the rate of absorption seems to be reduced."

Fizzy Drinks

Champagne goes straight to your head. The bubbles increase the rate of alcohol absorption because carbonation opens the pyloric sphincter, a strong ring of smooth muscle guarding the entrance to the small intestine, so the alcohol is absorbed more quickly. Conversely, ice-cold undiluted shots make the intestine seize up, so avoid sub-zero Stoli and say "hola" to Tequila slammers.

Mix Your Drinks

Mixing drinks (especially grape and grain) is renowned for producing a bigger hangover, but that's due to all the sugar in the juice and soda and because when you're on a binge, you are more likely to drink whatever is put in front of you. Also if you start by drinking beer, it's possible that when you switch to mixed drinks you might drink more because you've become accustomed to low alcohol content.

74. Crash a Closed Course :

Just because a course is closed doesn't mean you can't get into it. If you are organized, show commitment and passion, and have good people skills, you should be able to enrol in all your dream classes.

Register on Time

Even if a course is closed, the sooner your register the higher up the waiting list you will be. Make sure you don't have any outstanding tuition fees or library fines, which can delay your registration.

Be on Good Terms with Your Professors

Getting what you want is all about forming relationships, because paperwork, computers, and timetables don't get you what you want, people do. And people can always override systems, bend the rules, and get you into a closed course even when it is full. The professor can always get you into a course if they want, if you can convince them that you really want to be there.

Make a Convincing Case

If you want something bad enough, you can usually get it if you can convince those with the power to make it happen that you really, really want it. You will impress your professor with your passion for the course, and if you have a persuasive list of reasons why you want to take it, your commitment will be difficult to ignore. If you have to take a particular course this semester because it is vital for your major, say so. Make sure you have already fulfilled the prerequisites for the class you want, or get permission from the professor to bypass a prerequisite.

Maintain a Presence

Keep emailing the professor during the vacation to show him you are still interested, so if any places suddenly become available, he thinks of you. Email with the registrar regularly to check your position on the waiting list. Use all your charm with the registrar—people will bend over backwards to accommodate those who are charming and personable.

Auditing

If you are deadly serious about taking a particular course, then you should be prepared to audit it, that is, sit in on the classes even though you don't have to complete assignments and you don't get a grade. Even if you don't get graded this semester, if you get on the course next semester, you'll have a head start. Sometimes just starting to audit a class is enough to get you enrolled in it.

Crash the Class

Turn up on the first day of class and ask if you can sit in, then after class ask again if there are any free places; there are bound to be some no shows.

75. Ace a Multiple Choice Exam:

If you have studied, you will know many of the correct answers, so these techniques are to help you increase your odds of guessing the correct answer to questions that leave you clueless. Understanding how multiple choice tests are written can increase your success and to some extent allow you to reverse engineer the answer. Let's assume that each question contains four possible answers.

Question, Answer, Distracters

Consider for a moment how a professor works: first comes the question, but what next? Most probably it's the correct answer, followed by several wrong (or "nearly right") answers, called "distracters." This may seem self-evident, but going through this process can help you see relationships between right, wrong, and "nearly right" answers.

Paired Answers

There are different kinds of distracters. Some are clearly wrong (the professor doesn't

have the time to write three subtle distracters, so one
will probably be somewhat ridiculous and therefore easily
eliminated). That leaves the other two wrong answers which
are usually "nearly right," but one of them may actually point
you toward the correct answer. This is because there's a
strong chance that one of the "nearly right" distracters is
similar to the right answer. If you spot a pair of answers,
one is likely to be correct.

Spot Inconsistencies

Another way of eliminating distracters is to spot linguis-
tic or numerical inconsistencies between question and answers.
Remember, most of the professor's focus is directed toward
writing the question and making absolutely certain that a
correct answer is supplied. This means he or she may overlook
errors such as a singular question and plural distracter, a
difference in tense, or some other stylistic or grammatical
discrepancy.

"None of the Above" and "All of the Above"

These cover-alls often appear in multiple choice exams. The
first is usually wrong and the second is often correct. If "All
of the above" is wrong, this means the professor deliberately
decided to stay late to ensure the other two distracters are
significantly more plausible than usual.

76. Skip Classes:

Albert Einstein famously quipped, "the only reason for time is so that everything doesn't happen at all once." But as usual he was wrong. Stuff happens at once all the time, so when you've got some important sleeping or procrastination to do (re-alphabetizing your DVDs just can't wait another minute), sometimes skipping classes is the only way to stay on top of things (or underneath your duvet).

Stop the Guilt Trip

Your biggest obstacle to skipping class is probably you. A three-hour lecture has already cost your parents about $200 in tuition fees, but you won't get that money back regardless of whether you go to class, so ditch the burden and enjoy yourself. Besides, your myopic alcoholic professor doesn't take a roll-call, puts all his notes online, and doesn't know or care whether you attend, so stop beating yourself up. Ultimately, God is your judge and he would probably agree that your course sucks the big one. He also made the sun shine today, and if your professor wasn't so lame he would have cancelled the class anyway.

Lectures Are Boring

Ditching is an act of altruism—you'd only be a distraction to other students with your unnecessarily loud yawning, incessant fidgeting, flicking other people's ears, and staring out the window. Your college needs more people like you who deliberately place the public interest before your own; in fact they should be paying you to sleep in.

Find a Skip Mate

Choose a reliable "friend" with legible handwriting who always goes to lectures and takes notes, doesn't mind if you photocopy them, but doesn't realize that the only time you ever talk to them is to borrow work. They never miss a class, do they really expect to be able to hang out with a cool party animal like you?

Have a Good Excuse Ready

The next time you attend class have an excuse ready in case your professor puts you on the spot. Diarrhea, food poisoning, and unspecified visits to the doctor are weak and overused, so if you choose an ailment make it specific and slightly embarrassing to deter further probing—a toe infection, ingrown hair follicles, death of a family member, etc. Upbeat news is even better: a new baby in the family, you just tested negative for herpes, your father just got released on parole.

77. Get Away with Drinking in Class:

Oscar Wilde said that work was the curse of the drinking class, but what about drinking in class? One of the things that takes most students by surprise when they reach college is the number of petty rules that the professors have regarding behavior in class. At the beginning of the course when your professor lays down all the usual boring rules about no eating in class, no surfing the net, or shooting the breeze with your friends, if he or she makes a point of explicitly forbidding the drinking of alcohol in class, then you should sit up and listen.

No Drinking in Class

This must mean that a student, or more likely a bunch of them, in a previous class has not only drank, but has done so to such an extent that it has bugged the professor, and interfered with the lecture in some way. That's quite a lot of booze, because how many beers do you think you could put away before your professor would notice? Precisely. So respect is due to your predecessors, and also it seems a pity to let their efforts go to waste. They began, or were pursuing a drinking tradition; it is your duty to continue their good work. So if your professor says no, it is your duty to disobey.

Like It, Lump It, Ramp It

There can only be three reasons to drink in class: because you like the taste, the lecture is boring, or you and your friends are playing a game to see how much you can drink without getting caught, or passing out. Assuming the latter, the only way you can get some serious drinking done is to replace your bottled water with a colorless spirit such as gin, vodka, or ouzo. For a greater challenge, take a big slug while your professor is looking, or while you have your hand up to ask a question, and then try not to make a face as the liquor strips the skin off the inside of your throat.

Drink Along-a-Tic Game

Each person picks a word or two, and every time the professor says the word, that person has to take a drink. Or, if your professor has a tic or habit, everyone takes a swig every time it makes an appearance.

78. Construct and Use a Beer Bong:

Making and taking beer bongs is not only one of the most fun, efficient, and least labor-intensive ways of delivering beer to your stomach, it's also . . . nope, that's the only reason why it exists.

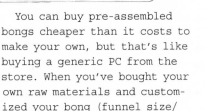

Materials

You can buy pre-assembled bongs cheaper than it costs to make your own, but that's like buying a generic PC from the store. When you've bought your own raw materials and customized your bong (funnel size/ tube width), it becomes a much-loved member of the family.

You should be able to get everything from the plumbing section of any hardware store. You'll need:

Funnel: translucent is best, so you can see the foam and clean it easily, and as large as possible (at least 2 beers worth). Try to find one with gradations on the side to show volume (if not, mark your own in ½ beer gradations with permanent marker).

Tubing: clear tubing, 2 to 2 ½ inches in diameter; this allows fast beer flow, but still fits comfortably in the mouth. The tubing should be about 3 feet long for individual use or unlimited if you have helpers (e.g. someone to hold and fill the bong out the second floor window while you stand on the ground below).

Turn valve: fits snugly into the tube to control flow.

Prepare the Bong

Open the valve and rinse the bong with ice cold water—this reduces foam build-up. Close the valve and, holding the funnel and tubing at 45 degrees, slowly pour the beer down the side of the funnel to minimize foam, then hold the apparatus vertical and allow any foam to settle until it has risen to the top of the funnel, or above the required gradation, or better yet, until all the bubbles have gone.

Now Take It

Assume the position (get down on one knee) and hold the funnel above your head with the tube vertical. Expel air from your mouth (i.e. depress your cheeks) and then place the end of the tube in your mouth (or if your name is Steve-O, your rectum). Open the valve. Don't suck. The best way is to open your throat and let gravity do its work; if you can't, remember to keep swallowing, rather than just let your mouth fill up.

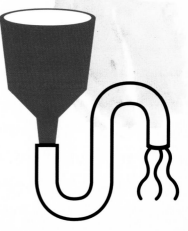

79. Organize a Campus Protest:

Students have it tough today with their racial and gender diversity, Wifi-enabled dorms, quad-core PCs, and 42-inch HD flat screen televisions. But if you look hard enough, you can always find something that makes you incensed enough to organize a campus protest. Here's how to make it a success.

Build Support

A lone voice can be power-ful, but there is strength in numbers. Use the Internet and social networking sites to promote your cause. Set up a website and a blog. Choose a time and place for your protest and post all the details on your communication channels. Make it clear to everyone that the protest must remain peaceful at all times.

Keep It Legal

Cities have many laws to restrict protests, but even at college you have to answer to the campus charter, and it's best to involve campus security and try to get the support of some faculty members to give your protest added legitimacy.

Invite the Media

Gain maximum attention for your cause by inviting the media. Also, just because your protest is peaceful doesn't mean you won't get your ass kicked, pepper sprayed, and arrested. On September 29, 2005, Tariq Khan, a junior at George Mason University in Virginia, stood four feet away from a Marine recruiter wearing a piece of paper taped to his chest bearing the words: "Recruiters Lie. Don't Be Deceived." He was violently arrested. That's why it's best to inform the media of your protest, so the campus police have an incentive to behave themselves and not wipe their asses all over the First Amendment. If you get closed down, your protest becomes a freedom of speech issue in the media.

Record the Event

Make sure that there is a visible presence of protestors and onlookers with cameras to deter inappropriate police action, and to record evidence if things turn nasty.

Follow Up

After the protest, update your social networks and blogs to tell everyone how it went, and to thank people for their support.

80. Get Off Paying Library Fines:

Everyone hates overdue charges. Not only do they hit your wallet, they also feel like a tax on your stupidity and lack of discipline. However, if your overdue library books are giving you sleepless nights, there are ways to beat the fine, which is often disproportionate and discriminates against the habitually disorganized.

Forge the Date Stamp

The date you checked out the book will be logged into the library's computer, as well as the return date. However, many libraries still use a crude system for recording this information inside the book, namely a date stamp label on the inside cover, or the half title page. These are extremely easy to forge. Simply scan in the label, erase all the date stamps in Photoshop, and then replace them all using the library stamper you picked up cheaply from eBay. Add one month to your own return date. The librarian will give you the benefit of the doubt and waive the fine, since only a real loser would go to all the trouble of forgery for the sake of a few cents.

Apply Game Theory

The Nash Equilibrium is a famous solution concept from Game Theory, a branch of applied mathematics that is used in the social sciences to analyze interactions between people based on the presumption that everyone acts in their own brazen self-interest. Nash Equilibrium is a state whereby two or more parties cannot benefit from changing their position unless the other parties also change. However, equilibrium does not always mean the best cumulative payoff for all the parties involved. The librarian serves his or her self-interest by sticking to the rules; if they waive the fine they risk getting fired, setting a precedent, or simply losing face. You serve your self-interest by not paying the fine. However, you can achieve an outcome that is better for both of you by threatening to beat up the librarian. The librarian's payoff changes to not getting punched in the face, while your payoff remains the same. Violence is great isn't it?

Reshelve the Books Yourself

If you don't want to resort to forgery or fighting, there is a third option. Don't check the books in, just reshelve them yourself. The next time you check out some books, the librarian will inform you that you have some overdue books, whereupon you explain that you have already returned them. A quick visit to the shelves will show that you are correct, and that the books have been accidentally reshelved without being scanned.

81. Persuade Your Professor to Bump Up Your Grades:

At the end of the semester, professors always get a rash of students who want to protest their grades. They've seen it all before, so they'll try to bullshit you with grading protocols and typical grade distribution, as if they haven't got any say or flexibility to bend the rules or listen to your case. They will hit you with these common objections, so here's how to handle them:

1. You have neither sought help during office hours nor contacted me to make an appointment for help.

- That's because I've had a huge crush on you so I tried to limit contact because I didn't know if I'd be able to resist hitting on you.

- That's because I have self-esteem issues, body odor, and sweat patches under my arms and I'm feeling suicidal right now. I don't leave my dorm very often. If you give me a bad grade, I might never venture out in public again.

- That's because I have been doing extra shifts at the homeless shelter. Those bums need me more than you.

2. There are grading protocols that I have to follow and the typical grade distribution shows that you deserve the C-minus I awarded you.

- But do I deserve to lose my scholarship and have to drop out of school?

- Don't you have any authority around here?

- I'm not a number.

3. Do you expect me to use different guidelines to grade you from those in the syllabus, and treat you differently from the other 180 people in your class?

- Yes and yes. One day I'll be so rich that I'll buy this college, sack you, and the only job you'll be able to get in this town will be jizz mopping.

4. Are you aware that seventy-five percent of the class earned a higher grade than you? Do you want me to bump them up too?

- Let's not cloud the issue by bringing in those losers. I don't care what you do with them. I just need a C to pass. Do you only take cash bribes or will you accept a blowjob with my compliments?

82. Read a Book Without Really Reading:

Do not confuse skim reading with speed reading. Speed reading is a technique which allows you to read more quickly without significantly reducing your comprehension and retention; skim reading allows your subconscious to assimilate the key ideas of a text. It is an emergency procedure to fool everyone in a seminar that you have read the assigned book.

Read the Introduction

Read the introduction; this will give you a good idea what the book is about, as well as several of the key themes. It may also give you some biographical information to drop into conversation during the seminar to show that you have boned up on the author's life.

First and Last

Read the first and last chapters of the books. The first chapter will set out the aims of the book (or if it's a novel, give you plenty of exposition); the last chapter will give you the conclusion.

Then go back and read the first and last two paragraphs of each chapter.

If you have time, read the first and last sentence of each paragraph. Highlight anything important and make margin notes of your immediate thoughts (a heavily annotated book looks well-thumbed).

If it's a textbook, read the titles, subtitles, subheadings, and illustration captions. Look out for dates, names, and places and examine graphs, tables, and charts.

Distress and Personalize Your Book

Batter your book to make it look like it hasn't left your side for two weeks. Crease the cover and spill coffee on it. With paperbacks, bend the spine back in several places until you hear a crack. If you have time, letting it sit out in the sun makes it look like a much perused and treasured possession.

83. Pull an All-Nighter for a Big Test:

Pulling an all-nighter is a great way to rescue your grades when you've been partying hard and neglecting your studies. The usefulness of an all-nighter is dependent on your ability to sustain effective concentration, so everything you do should further this goal. Your aim is NOT to stay awake at your desk fooling yourself you are working—you must make maximum use of the available time.

Eliminate Distractions

Switch off everything that could distract you—cell phone, TV, radio, talking cookie jar, and unplug your router so you won't be tempted to check your email or search for midget porn—five minutes on Facebook or playing Red Remover (green shapes are lovely) quickly turns into one hour. If you work better with music, turn it down and choose fast-paced and dissonant tunes from the Chemical Brothers or Einsturzende Neubauten, rather than a Mozart yawn-fest because slow harmonic music slows down your heartbeat, makes you drowsy, and encourages the wearing of suede elbow patches.

Structure Your Time

Try to work for fifty minutes, and then take ten minutes off—stick to this pattern for the whole night. Wash your hands and splash your face with cold water before resuming work. This rigid structure will help to maintain momentum, which can be easily lost.

Food and Drink

Avoid coffee, energy drinks, and caffeine pills, which keep you awake and buzzed at the expense of being able to concentrate. Stimulants increase anxiety levels and may even tip you into feeling overwhelmed by the task ahead. Instead, drink a glass of ice cold water every half hour. Avoid sugary foods, which will give you a quick burst of energy and then bring you crashing down again. Carbs will also make you sleepy, so choose protein-rich foods instead.

Temperature

Open a window to allow plenty of cold fresh air into your room. Turn up the air conditioning until the temperature is cold enough to keep you alert but comfortable.

Lighting

Use lighting bright enough to keep you alert, but not so bright that it gives you a headache or strains your eyes. Set your monitor brightness accordingly.

Body Position

Sit up straight. Slouching not only makes you feel tired, it is also a more stressful position for your body to maintain. Sit on a chair and work at a desk. Don't work in bed, and if possible, keep your bed out of your sightline.

Power Nap

When you hit a complete slump, set an alarm for fifteen minutes and take a power nap, but only if you are totally whacked out.

Stay Positive

Treat the experience as an adventure, rather than a chore, and remain upbeat. Whenever your mind begins to wander, or you start having negative thoughts, bring your focus back to the work and how well you are doing.

84. Get an Extension on Your Paper:

Persuading your professor to give you an extension on an assignment doesn't need to be an exercise in losing face and admitting defeat. You can use the encounter to make a positive impression, despite the fact that you have missed the original deadline.

Accentuate the Positive

Explain to your professor that your paper is going very well so far, and you are very pleased with the results, but that you need extra time to really do it justice. This stresses your desire to achieve excellence and draws attention away from your poor time management. Don't complain, make excuses, or put yourself down by saying how many other projects are competing for your attention or how bad you are at hitting deadlines. The professor doesn't care about your other work. Project an image of dedication, focus, and enthusiasm.

Rave about the Subject

Say that you spent too much time researching because you are so fascinated and enthused by the subject (your professor shares your passion, remember) that unfortunately you haven't left yourself enough time for writing it. Stress that your finished paper will be of the highest standard (you've got to back this up with genuinely impressive results).

Ask Questions

Ask some intelligent and searching questions that are relevant to your assignment, and try to engage your prof in fervent discussion about the topic. This portrays you as a motivated and talented student with a bright and enquiring mind. Not only is she likely to grant you an extension, it will actually boost her opinion of you.

Deliver the Paper Before the New Deadline

If you are given an extra week, hand in your paper two days early. This shows that not only can you keep a deadline, you can do better. Although you have effectively delivered five days late, the professor will remember that you delivered two days earlier than required, suggesting that you haven't taken the extension for granted.

85. Swallow a Goldfish:

On March 3, 1939, a Harvard freshman, Lothrop Withington Jr., chewed and then swallowed a three-inch live goldfish in the dining hall of the Freshmen Union for $10 in front of his fellow students. He then took a toothbrush from his pocket and after cleaning his teeth declared, "the scales caught a bit on my throat as it went down."

The Birth of a Craze

Withington's antics sparked intercollegiate rivalry followed by a nationwide college craze, as undergraduates tried to outdo each other by swallowing ever increasing numbers of goldfish in one sitting. First Frank Hope Jr. at Franklin and Marshall College in Lancaster, Pennsylvania swallowed three goldfish (without chewing). Harvard retaliated when Irving Clark Jr. swallowed two dozen goldfish, and then other colleges joined in. Albert Haynes at MIT consumed forty-two fish, and Joseph Deliberato from Clark University scarfed eighty-nine. Finally the Massachusetts state legislature passed a bill outlawing the practice, and the craze eventually died out, to emerge sporadically in later decades. By the 1970s, the record was more than 300 fish.

Dry Run

Plunge your hand into the tank and catch the fish's tail between your thumb and forefinger. Tilt your head back and try to open your throat. Goldfish-eating newbies usually have to employ some form of liquid lubricant to ease the passage of the fish down the throat. However, a purist would argue that the fish should be swallowed whole (chewing optional) and only afterwards should a beverage be drank. Fish are slimy, so it should slip down without much fuss so long as you remain relaxed. Follow up with a double-shot of whiskey to get your throat burning. This should rid your mouth and throat of the slippery fish sensation, and you'll be so busy gagging on the shot that you won't be thinking about anything else.

Waterfall

The easiest way to chug a fish is to place it inside a glass of water and then swallow the water and fish together.

What Happens Next

The acid in your stomach will quickly kill the goldfish. However, the story doesn't end there. You can catch some nasty diseases from this trick, like anaemia or a tapeworm.

86. Survive a Meningitis Outbreak:

Bacterial meningitis is relatively rare and usually occurs in isolated cases, nevertheless it kills about 1,000 people in the United States each year. In order to survive an outbreak you must do three things: avoid people who have the infection, maintain good personal hygiene, and, most importantly, recognize the symptoms so you can seek immediate treatment.

Recognize the Symptoms

There are two kinds of meningitis, the viral form and the deadly bacterial form. Many people carry and spread viral meningitis without experiencing any symptoms. The symptoms are similar for both forms, but most cases of viral meningitis are mild and clear up without treatment within a few weeks. Symptoms include headaches, fever, a stiff neck, sensitivity to light, nausea and vomiting, diarrhea, confusion and drowsiness, and weight loss. If you have these symptoms, see a physician immediately; if you have bacterial meningitis you need to begin a course of antibiotics immediately to stand a chance of full recovery.

Bacterial Meningitis

This is a serious infection of the fluid in the spinal cord and the fluid that surrounds the brain. It is commonly caused by one of three types of bacteria: Haemophilus influenzae type b (Hib), Neisseria meningitidis, or Streptococcus pneumoniae. If you have aching limbs, joint pain, cold hands and feet, and a pin prick rash and bruising, you may have developed Meningococcal septicaemia, which can also be fatal if untreated. Advanced bacterial meningitis or Meningococcal septicaemia can lead to brain damage, coma, and death, or long term complications, including hearing loss, paralysis, and seizures.

Wash Your Hands

Something as simple as washing your hands before eating and after using the restroom can greatly reduce your chances of infection. Don't share food or dining ware such as cups, plates, and cutlery. Don't even share someone else's lip balm. In fact, if one of your friends gets bacterial meningitis, rush them to the hospital then burn all their stuff and head for the hills.

87. Tell If You've Got Alcohol Poisoning:

Alcohol poisoning and alcohol poisoning symptoms occur when someone drinks more than their body is able to metabolize (i.e. break down and eliminate from the body). Each year in the United States, 50,000 people suffer alcohol poisoning, and one person dies from it each week. If you suspect you or someone you know has alcohol poisoning dial 9-1-1 and ask for immediate medical help (don't wait for all the symptoms below to appear). Diagnosing yourself when you are dangerously drunk can be very difficult, (impossible if you are unconscious), so recognizing the signs early, and cooperating with those who are trying to help you is paramount.

Your Blood Alcohol Level

Many factors affect your blood alcohol level, and the effect of alcohol in your body, including the strength of the alcohol, the quantity and speed with which you drink, how quickly your body metabolizes alcohol, how much food is in your stomach, your sex, and your body weight.

Booze and Drugs

Don't be fooled into ruling out the possibility of alcohol poisoning simply because someone hasn't drank very much. Alcohol poisoning symptoms can occur with a relatively low intake of alcohol, when mixed with recreational drugs or other drugs such as pain medication, sedatives, and certain anti-seizure medications (such as phenobarbital).

Tossing Your Cookies

Feeling sick or being sick are very clear signs of alcohol poisoning, but just because you threw up doesn't mean that you are out of danger. The level of alcohol in your blood may already be at a dangerous level. Other symptoms include: absent reflexes, slurred speech, inability to feel pain, seizures, erratic behavior, severe confusion, irregular breathing (fast or slow), blueish or pale skin, even heavier vomiting, very low body temperature, or falling unconscious. If someone shows any of these signs before they "fall asleep," they aren't "just sleeping it off."

Just Sleeping It Off

Just because someone is sleeping doesn't mean they don't have alcohol poisoning; they may stop breathing or choke on their own vomit (because their gag reflex is suppressed), and their blood alcohol levels may still be rising. If someone vomits while asleep, turn them onto their side so they don't choke and try to revive them. If they can't be woken up, they may have slipped into a coma.

88. Grow Marijuana in Your Dorm Room:

Growing marijuana indoors is harder than growing it outside. It requires at least eight hours of sunlight every day. However, it has the advantage of being concealed from nosey law enforcers like your RA and the cops, both of whom will take it off you and smoke it themselves. If you think about it for a moment, it won't surprise you to learn that marijuana is a weed. This means that it grows like . . . well, like a weed, as long as you provide the right conditions.

Plant Your Seeds

Soak your nice green seeds (if they are gray, they won't work) overnight in distilled water, and then plant them ½ inch deep with the pointy end up in an indoor starter box to germinate. The growing medium should be a mixture of fertilizer, soil, compost, and sand, so that it absorbs water well.

Transplant

When the sprouts are well established, transplant them into grow bags, allowing about one cubic foot of soil per plant and space the plants at least two feet apart. Make sure you leave plenty of soil around the roots, so you don't damage them. Water well before and after transplanting.

Ambient Conditions

The temperature around the plant should not exceed 75 degrees. Provide up to sixteen hours of "sunlight" (with a minimum of eight hours) each day using a 75 watt fluorescent strip light positioned about 1½ feet from the plants. Cover your dorm walls behind the plants with aluminum foil to reflect the light. Keep the room well ventilated.

Harvesting

Your crop will produce both male and female plants, both of which contain THC (the major psychoactive chemical compound, tetrahydrocannabinol). The male plants are generally tall with stout stems and a few leaves, and they have little buds which look like little nuts. The females just have white pubes. Harvest the male plants before they shed their pollen (unless you want the female to produce seeds). If the female plant is not pollinated, its flower will continue to grow and produce more THC than if it were allowed to produce seeds. Cut the plants at soil level.

Curing

Before you can smoke your weed, it must be dried. Place the leaves on a baking sheet and bake in the middle of a hot oven until they smoke and curl up. Remove them from the oven and store them somewhere cool until you are ready to get high.

89. Run a Wet T-shirt Competition:

Wet T-shirt competitions are sexy, sexist, and lots of fun. When H_2O and gazungas get together the results are always spectacular.

Find a Venue

You'll attract more people to your event (and more hot chicks prepared to get their tits soaked) if you approach a local bar and ask them to host it. They may even agree to give a free drink to each ticket holder, since they increase their take behind the bar.

Set a Date

If you plan to make this a regular event, keep the same day every week, or month, or whatever, so people know that Friday night is hooters night. The best time is late evening, around midnight, when plenty of alcohol has been consumed and people are feeling less inhibited.

Promote the Event

Charge a participation fee, sell tickets, hand out special-offer flyers, and put up a generous cash prize for first, second, and third place.

Prevent Lawsuits

All contestants must show picture ID proving that they are legally old enough to take part, and get them to sign an entry form which acknowledges their age, and absolving you of liability if they get injured or if photos or videos of them appear on the Internet or anywhere else. Just in case don't let anyone in the audience take photos or video—and watch out for cell phones. Make sure the stage is covered with a rubber mat or some other non-slippery surface, so no one slips and sues you for their injuries. Also, make sure water doesn't get anywhere near the electronic devices, or you could have an electrocution injury, a fire, or a power outage.

Secure the Staging Area

Make sure you've got some big tough guys to protect the contestants and prevent anyone from jumping onto the stage. Make
it clear to the audience at the start that they will be thrown
out if they try to grope or harass the girls.

Judging

The winner is usually the person who gets the most applause
and cheers from the audience, but you can formalize the event
by having a panel of judges. See if you can get a celebrity to
be one of the judges, to help draw a crowd. Invite the local
radio DJ to be another judge, so he'll promote the event on
his show. Make sure you're one of the judges, so you get the
best view and maybe even a few telephone numbers afterwards.

90. Recognize When You've Been Given GHB:

Gamma-hydroxybutyric acid, better known as GHB, is the one of the most commonly used date-rape drugs, along with Rohypnol and Ketamine. It's a general anesthetic, but very difficult to detect because it is colorless, practically odorless, and

its taste is easily disguised when added to food or drink, so recognizing the symptoms can help to keep you safe. In small quantities it occurs naturally in the human brain and central nervous system as well as in wine, beef, and small citrus fruits. So if your date plies you with a 2lb steak and Satsuma sauce, call the cops and get out of there.

Body Signs

Initially GHB reduces your anxiety, makes you feel relaxed and less inhibited, and often drowsy. Identical symptoms are created by drinking alcohol, so if you are drinking but you feel more drunk than your alcohol intake warrants, this may be a sign you've been slipped GHB. Other symptoms include a slowing heart rate and nausea.

Smell Your Drink

GHB is largely odourless, but if you have a keen sense of smell you may be able to detect a whiff of gas, or a salty "chemical" odor.

The Morning After

A GHB hangover is similar to an alcohol hangover—headaches, nausea, upset stomach, increased heart rate, high blood pressure, increased sweating, and in very severe cases, hallucinations. GHB also messes with your memory, so you can't rely on it to tell you what really happened.

Check out your genitals for abrasions. If your combined symptoms lead you to suspect date rape, don't wash or shower—go straight to the cops to give swabs and a urine sample immediately, since GHB is undetectable within twenty-four hours.

91. Challenge a Dorm Damage Report:

When challenging a dorm report, don't make the mistake of trying to shift responsibility on to someone else. Don't blame it on the sunshine, the moonlight, the good times, or even the boogie. Instead, you need to discredit the report and the person who made it (your RA), and then commission one of your own. If that doesn't work, blame society, the global downturn, or your kid brother.

Discredit the Damage Report

Launch a diplomatic offensive to undermine the credibility of the damage report and then follow this up with false allegations about your RA. Appear on network TV and read out this statement, which contains all the key phrases trotted out by politicians when they want to ignore reports: "This damage report sets a dangerous precedent. It leaves important questions unanswered, much of the evidence is inconclusive, the findings are open to other interpretations, certain findings are contradictory, and some of its main conclusions have been questioned."

Discredit Your RA

Wage a propaganda war against your RA. Appear on network TV and read out this statement: "I believe the RA is harboring a grudge against me and other members of my dorm; he is a publicity seeker who is trying to boost his own profile so he can run for local government, or become a consultant to a multinational financial organization. He is conducting an improper relationship with the residential director, has a drinking problem, and believes in UFOs."

Commission Your Own Report

Commission an independent report into the dorm damage but limit its scope so it can only examine who ripped the stitching in the arm of the couch, and is not able to investigate who kicked holes in the drywall, stole the curtains, and took a dump on the pool table. While the report is taking place, tell everyone that you can't comment because it would be "foolish" of you "to pre-empt the findings of the report." The report will take years, and when it finally comes out, you will have graduated and can say that now is not the time to look back, everyone must look to the future. If you have managed to start a war in the interim, you can say that challenging the dorm report now in unpatriotic and will cost lives, so say it's everyone's duty to admire the new furniture, rather than try to figure out who knocked the crap out of the old stuff.

92. Kick Ass at Beer Pong:

Not content to be losing the war against drugs, and the ones in the Middle East, the powers that be are now waging war against our national pastime. If your university has recently banned beer pong, then even playing the game poorly is sticking up for your civil rights, so well done. However, if you want to be the best beat the best, here are a few beer pong insider techniques. Please drink irresponsibly and be the sorest loser whenever you're kicked off the table.

The Rules

Rules are made to be broken, and there are so many variations that it is only worth stating the aim of the game here: two sets of ten cups containing beer are placed on both ends of a table in a triangular formation, like bowling pins. Teams take turns trying to throw or bounce a ping pong ball into their opponent's cups. The other team must drink whatever cups the ball lands in and remove the cup from play. The object is to take out all the opposing team's cups, whereupon they must drink all of the winning team's remaining cups.

Hand-Eye Coordination

It may not have occurred to you that this game is all about hand-eye coordination, which is one of the first things that suffers when you've had a few drinks. Therefore it follows that if you want to win a beer pong series, you really have to focus hard on the first few games—the more beer you can make your opponents drink early on, the worse they will play. If you have a good run at the beginning, they'll soon be too drunk to get back in the game (especially if you've spiked their cups with vodka).

Grips and Releases

Most players simply grip the ball between their thumb, index and middle fingers, and then release the ball quickly and smoothly with a slight snap of the wrist. There is no correct way to hold or release the ball, but it is worth experimenting with different grips to see which suits you best:

Hooked Overhand: hold the ball between your thumb tip and your hooked index finger. Aim by lining up your thumb with the first knuckle of your finger. Snap your wrist as you release to give the ball a little topspin.

Reverse Overhand: hold the ball between the tips of all your digits, with your palm up. Flick your hand forward and release.

Screw You: make a V sign with your index and middle fingers and grip ball between the fingertips. Flick your hand forward while spreading your fingers to release.

Feet Placement

Don't stand with your feet lined up with the cups; if you throw with your right hand, stand off-center with your right foot lined up with the cups, just as you would for throwing free shots in basketball.

Aim for a Single Cup

Beginners focus on all the cups and aim somewhere toward the middle. However, even when there are several cups on the table, it is better to aim for one cup. This means that by the time the cups are thinned down, you are already focused on single cups and won't have to switch gears; it also improves your accuracy over time.

Raise Your Arc

Balls with a low trajectory have to be thrown faster than those with a high arc, which means they deflect more often, even though you may achieve more knocked over cups (if the House Rules allow those to count). However, your balls-sunk average will generally be higher if you use a medium or high arc.

93. Avoid Being Scammed by a Bartender:

There are dozens of bartender scams. Here are six of the most common.

Short Changing

Counting your change is inconvenient, and bartenders know it. Always take a few seconds to count your change, and if you suspect the bartender is short changing you, make a point of doing it while he is watching, so he knows you're onto him and won't risk it again.

Top Shelf Switcheroo

You pay extra for a top-shelf drink, but instead of getting premium vodka, the bartender pours you a regular shot from one of the standard bottles and pockets the difference. Never order a top-shelf drink unless you can see the bartender pour your drink. You're most likely to get scammed like this in a joint with waitress service.

Fat Tab

Before you start a tab, check with the bartender to see if the drinks will be itemized at the end of the night. If not, pay a round at a time. Otherwise, come the end of the night when everyone is drunk and no one can remember how many drinks they had, you won't notice the few extra drinks that have made their way onto your bill.

Cost Jumping

The bartender charges different prices to different customers for the same drink. If regulars are getting their drinks cheaper than you, then your inflated prices may be subsidizing them because the bartender has to balance the books—otherwise his boss will know what he's been up to. If this happens to you, order a different kind of drink (the bartender won't be able to pull this scam on every type of drink, as straight drinks are easier to audit than those with a high spillage rate like beer). If that doesn't work, go somewhere else.

Drink Shortening

There are plenty of ways of shortening a drink, but the most extreme version is to give you no shot at all. Say you order a gin and tonic. All the bartender has to do to convince you that your drink has gin in it is to dip the rim into a saucer of gin, then add the ice, tonic, and pretend to pour the gin (keeping thumb over the spout). When you drink you'll taste and inhale the gin on the rim, but you'll have been scammed.

Chipped Bottle

If you're sold a drink in a chipped bottle, ask for another one. Not only are you risking cutting yourself or even swallowing glass (since the glass chip may have fallen inside the bottle), the bartender may already have shown it to the boss and had it marked down as waste, meaning that every penny you pay him is going into his pocket.

94. Get Rid of Dorm Odors:

The world around us is filled with odors. Some of them smell pleasant and make us feel good, while others are rank and make us want to hurl. It is important to eliminate bad dorm odors because unpleasant smells adversely affect our mood as much as pleasant ones can make us feel energized, happy, and positive. Fortunately, there are lots of ways to freshen a smelly dorm, without using commercial air freshening products which are full of nasty chemicals and can cause allergies and asthma.

Find the Source

The best way to eliminate odors is to find the source and clean it if possible (e.g. dirty laundry, moldy food) or introduce something to neutralize the odor (e.g. inside sneakers).

Baking Soda

Baking soda (sodium hydrogen carbonate or sodium bicarbonate, $NaHCO_3$) is a weak alkali, so it has the effect of neutral-

izing the acids and bases which cause the bad smells.
Dissolve it in warm water and use it to clean your fridge,
or any non-porous surface, or sprinkle it dry onto carpets,
or put a small bag of baking soda inside your sneakers when
you aren't wearing them.

Charcoal

Poke several holes in the lid of an empty shoe box, fill it
with charcoal, and then leave the box wherever you want to neutralize nasty odors (ground coffee or plain clay cat litter will
also work). Alternatively, fill a nylon stocking with charcoal and
hang it somewhere in your room. The charcoal will trap parti-
cles that carry the compounds that make the smells.

White Vinegar

Fill a deodorizer spray with white vinegar and spray a
little into the air, or spray it onto something that stinks.
(It's very good and getting rid of urine smells.)

Vanilla Extract

Take a cotton ball and soak it with vanilla extract. Leave
the cotton ball anywhere where bad odors linger. If you have a
microwave in your dorm, put 3 teaspoons of vanilla extract in
a saucer and zap it in your microwave for one minute. You can
even dab a couple drops of it on your light bulbs.

95. Hack the Library Computers:

According to records kept by OpenDNS's domain filtering tool, the ten most-blocked websites by parents, schools, colleges, and small businesses are:

1. MySpace.com

2. Facebook.com

3. YouTube.com

4. Playboy.com

5. Ebay.com

6. Meebo.com

7. Friendster.com

8. Orkut.com

9. AdultFriendFinder.com

10. Espn.com

Annoying isn't it? If your college library routinely blocks scores of websites that are essential for your sanity, including outside emailing tools like hotmail.com, it will either use filtering software or have a list of blocked sites in a hosts file. Fortunately, both of these systems are ripe for hacking.

Use the IP Address

The simplest way to bypass domain name based filtering protocols is to use the direct numerical IP address, which you can find by using an online conversion tool such as *www.hcidata.info/host2ip.htm.*

If the library also blocks access to conversion sites, then you must ping the site directly to get the IP address.

1. Open the command window by clicking START, then RUN. Type CMD and hit Enter or click OK. If the system doesn't allow you to do this, create a cmd.bat file (see below) to open the command window.

2. Type "ping" and hit the space bar.

3. Type the website address that you want to ping (e.g. hotmail.com) and hit Enter.

4. The server will return various data including the IP address (e.g. 64.4.32.7 is the IP address of hotmail.com).

5. Type the IP address directly into your web browser and hit Enter.

Edit the Hosts File

If the system keeps a list of blocked sites in a hosts file, you can edit it as follows:

1. Open the command window by clicking START, then RUN. Type CMD and hit Enter or click OK. If the system doesn't allow you to do this, create a cmd.bat file (see below) to open the command window.

2. Type: start c://windows/system32/drivers/etc

3. This will open a folder containing several files. Find the one called "hosts" and open it in Wordpad.

4. Scroll down to find and remove the sites you want to visit.

5. Save the file, and close the command window.

Create a cmd.bat File

1. Open Notepad and type "cmd.exe".

2. Save the file to the desktop and call it cmd.bat

3. Double-click on your newly created file to open the command prompt.

96. Passed Out Buddy Ownage:

At the dawn of time when the first caveman lost consciousness after binging on rotten fruit, his friends and family were probably too stunned to think of piling rocks on his chest or shaving off his pubes, and it was thousands of years before the invention of the Sharpie and YouTube. Thankfully the human race has come a long way since then. Today there are probably three main areas of ownage: drawing, taping, and balancing objects—but the only limit is your imagination.

Sharpie Fun

Classic ownage usually involves a Sharpie marker, but if you don't want to get too permanent, toothpaste is a versatile medium too. The face is the most obvious target. Sharpie modifications include moustaches and unibrows. But don't neglect the torso. Decorate an entire naked upper torso by drawing a dress shirt, wing collar, and bowtie (and don't forget the pocket square). There's nothing worse than passing out and missing all the fun, but just because someone is unconscious doesn't mean they can't take part in some party games—you can play Tic-Tac-Toe or Hangman on all areas of visible skin.

Face Tape

Duct tape, clear tape, masking tape—doesn't matter. Don't tape eyes open, or they'll dry out and get damaged. Make sure you leave open the airways (nose and mouth). If you're taping the body, be aware of whether your subject will be able to break their fall if they roll off the bed/couch.

Balancing

Balancing stuff raises ownage several notches by testing the structural engineering skills and hand-eye coordination of those who are still conscious. Objects can range in size from beer cans to tables and chairs.

Breakfast in Bed

What's colorful, messy, and smelly? Food, which is why it's so good for ownage because it's cheap, available, and appeals to several senses at once. Who doesn't love waking up to breakfast in bed? Pour an entire box of breakfast cereal over your buddy's head, followed by a glass of milk, and sugar if you like. If he is still hungry, follow it up with a stack of pancakes and a cup of lukewarm coffee.

Pool Raft

Do not do this. Your friend will drown. This is probably the most famous viral ownage video (for entertainment purposes only): *www.youtube.com/watch?v=l8vQVZXtNoM*

A bunch of guys drag their passed out buddy onto a pool raft and push him out into the middle of a pond. Finally one of them figures out the danger: "How has he not woken up? He's soaked . . . Hey, hey, you guys realize if this raft tips and he doesn't wake up, one of us is going in after him." They start hurling stuff at him and then at 2:37 he finally wakes up . . . check out the link to see if he survives.

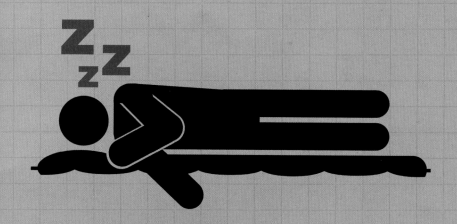

97. Ruin Your Roommate's Life:

Here are the seven habits of highly irritating people. If these don't drive your roommate crazier than a fish with titties, nothing will.

1. Hide underwear in his closet and then accuse him of having a panty-sniffing fetish. When he owns up and begs you to keep it a secret, tell him you planted the evidence and that he has just given away far too much information.

2. Fire off a party popper every time he comes back to the dorm and say, "this calls for a celebration" then burst into tears and confess how much you value his companionship.

3. Cut off some of his hair while he is asleep and leave it for him to find. Repeat every night for a week, and then show him your fake CNN report about Russian terrorists hiding radioactive isotopes in goose-down pillows.

4. Sleepwalk. Pad around the room quietly, and then pretend to have a night terror, groan loudly starting

quiet and low and ending loud and high in a "they're-coming-to-get-me" style. Jump back under your covers and start snoring.

5. Get him to sign a contract agreeing to divide the room down the middle, and that you will respect each other's personal space by asking permission to cross into their territory. Make sure your half of the room contains the door. For the next year insist that he ask your permission to enter and exit the room.

6. Collect plush toys and talk to them like they all have individual little personalities.

7. Finish all your sentences with the words "in accordance with prophecy."

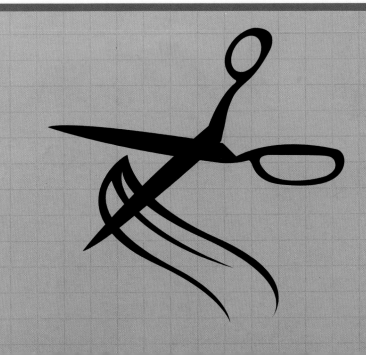

— 98. Pass a Drug Test:

The best way to pass a drug test is not to take one in the first place, but if your college or employer puts you on the spot, there are a few ways for a dope head to escape detection.

Jell-O Drink-

This trick works only for fat-soluble drugs such as marijuana, heroin, and PCP, which means that they get stored in your fat cells. You can also disguise fat soluble steroids this way, but not completely. Don't try this if you are diabetic.

1. Dissolve a whole packet of Jell-O into half a glass of water and shake well. Don't put the solution into the refrigerator as you don't want the Jell-O to set; you want to be able to drink it.

2. Drink three glasses of tap water, or as much as it takes you to pee once or twice before the test.

3. Fifteen minutes before the test, drink the Jell-O solution. This will flood your body with sugar, so your body won't have to metabolize the oil in your fat cells to create energy.

Other sample spiking or masking products will also work, such as Mary Jane Super Clean 13 (liquid soap), Urinaid (glutaraldehyde), Klear (nitrite), but the testers now test with these products too.

Dilute the Sample

If you have access to warm water, you can dilute the sample to reduce concentration of the drug. This will work for performance enhancing drugs such as creatine that naturally occur in the body, but not for recreational drugs which shouldn't be there in the first place. Most testing facilities are wise to this, so they dye toilet water, and block access to other sources of water.

Switch the Sample

Switch your sample with one belonging to someone else, or use synthetic urine from a laboratory supplier. These come in either concentrated liquid or powdered form—just add warm water (92 degrees) and hide in a tiny thermos flask until required. The powdered form is better because the liquid form has no smell.

Shave Your Hair

Drugs leave their signature in your hair for years afterwards (it reaches the hair follicles through the blood vessels), so shave your head, armpits, pubes, chest, and legs to a length of no longer than half an inch (one inch is the minimum length of hair required for successful testing). Bleaching or dying your hair will not disguise the drugs.

Saliva Test

If you are asked to provide a sample of saliva or other oral fluids, despite all your previous preparations, you are screwed.

99. Write Your Valedictorian Speech:

Congratulations for having cheated in every exam or hacking into the college computers to give yourself the highest GPA. Now all you have to do is deliver a valedictorian speech they'll never forget. Great valedictory speeches follow a pattern. They say how great college was, they use lots of lame motivational quotations and anecdotes about being the best and seizing the day, they offer advice, and they mention a few teachers and fellow students so everyone feels included by proxy. Just cobble together the best parts of some famous speeches and tweak to make relevant to your college.

My fellow graduates: I stand here today humbled by the task before us, grateful for the trust you have bestowed, mindful of the sacrifices borne by our parents, and I take pride in the words "Ich bin ein [insert name of any jelly-filled confection]. I thank [insert name of Dean] for his/her service to our college, as well as the [insert two nouns] s/he has shown throughout the last four years.

During our time here we have learned a lot. We have learned [insert a serious example]; we have learned [insert a hokey example]; we have learned that [insert lame joke example]. But above all we have learned [insert sanctimonious and syrupy anecdote that will make everyone look at the person next to them and nod sagely].

That we are in the midst of crisis is now well understood. Our nation is at war, against a far-reaching network of violence and hatred. Our economy is badly weakened, a consequence of greed and irresponsibility on the part of some, but also our collective failure to make hard choices and prepare the nation for a new age.

So, first of all, let me assert my firm belief that the only thing we have to fear is fear itself. Over the next few minutes, I'd like to talk about what we've learned, the people we have to thank, and the people we have to remember [insert yet more bullshit about what you've learned personally, thank some people, and then bum everyone out by getting them to reflect on any students or teachers who have died]. The world will little note nor long remember what you say here but it can never forget what they did here.

The rest of us are now graduates. [Now you've got them feeling depressed, make them blub by talking about saying goodbyes and keeping in touch. Pretend to break down, then compose yourself and continue.] As a final thought going forward, I'd like to leave you with a quote from [insert name of your granny/father/dead mother, etc.] who always told me [insert cloying quote from Oprah or Dr. Phil].

And so even though we face the difficulties of today and tomorrow, I still have a dream. It is a dream deeply rooted in the American dream. From every mountainside, let freedom ring. Free at last! Free at last! Class of [insert year], we are free at last!

100. Stand Out at a Career Fair:

You'll face many challenges during your college career—sitting through a two-hour lecture with a hangover without dry heaving or falling asleep; dating three people at once; funneling four beers in a row—but nothing can quite prepare you for the existential horror of the job fair.

Negative Process

Unlike many times in life when people try to see the best in each other, job fairs turn this principle on its head due to logistic pressures. Companies are looking for reasons to screen you out in order to whittle down their list of graduates, so first impressions really count.

Practice Standing in Line

You will spend most of your time standing in line, waiting to hand your resume to recruiters. It's a test. The way people perform this acquired social trait speaks volumes about their personality and employability. Recruiters can quickly weed out those who shuffle from foot to foot (impatient/poor circulation); stand patiently (ex-Communists used to bread lines);

or place weight on the balls of the feet with knees flexed, hands about chest high with elbows bent and arms close to their sides (basketball dropouts). Line up the American way: talk loudly and confidently to your friend over the heads of other people in the line.

Do Something Unexpected

Jump in the air, throw some gang signs, play a practical joke on someone, start speaking in tongues, remove all your skin with a toothpick, run with a pair of scissors, convert your nipples into smoke detectors, count out loudly how many times you blink, whatever you do obey the little voice in your head.

World of Warcraft

You have the technical skills, the quantitative know-how, a high GPA, and strong communication skills, but the biggest buzzword now in business is globalization. The big companies, investment banks, and consulting firms are looking for people who can function globally. A good degree with overseas work experience is all well and good, but the real clincher is the status of your *World of Warcraft* guild, with which you can demonstrate strategic thinking, global experience, complicated multi-phase battling as well as a sharp full suit of Dark Iron Plate. It doesn't matter that you have acquired all your assets through hours of moronic gold farming, and that you are essentially unemployable because of recurrent RSI in your mouse arm, find someone in the company who plays WOW and they will be your entry ticket. Try to talk personally with a representative at each individual company, and show them your personal collection of screen grabs from Onyxia's Lair.

101. Sue Your Alma Mater When You Can't Get a Job:

Suing your college on account of the fact that you can't find work for full reimbursement plus compensation for emotional distress—that's ridiculous, right? When you go to college there is no guarantee that you're going to get a job, especially in today's marketplace where a college degree is the bare minimum employers expect. A liberal arts education is supposed to make you a more rounded and engaged citizen, it's not guaranteed to get you work, but you know . . . what the hell, this is America!

File for Poor Person Status

As a fully unemployed recent graduate, you won't have the money to pay filing fees and costs associated with a lawsuit, so you should apply for an order designating you as a "poor person" before you start your action. This will exempt you from paying costs, and taxpayers will have to pick up the tab. You must submit an affidavit which proves that you're broke. If the judge grants the order you can start your action without paying any initial fees or court costs, but as your case progresses you will have to find money to pay other expenses, so the sooner you plea bargain or find a job, the better.

Settle Out of Court

To be honest, your chances of winning your action aren't good. Cases like yours generally bomb because courts do not recognize educational malpractice as a tort. So your best chance is to settle out of court. You'd have more chance of winning if you spilled coffee in your lap and then sued your college for not offering classes on the inherent dangers of scolding beverages. If you are a law graduate, you could make a lukewarm case that you should now be more aware of the folly of spurious litigation.

While settling out of court is far less expensive than a trial, you will still need to shell out between $50 to $400 an hour for a trained mediator who can help you reach a fair and legally binding "mediation agreement" which you can then enforce in court if your college doesn't pay up.